HELMSHORE

EDITED AND COMPILED BY
CHRIS ASPIN, DEREK PILKINGTON AND JOHN SIMPSON

HELMSHORE LOCAL HISTORY SOCIETY

SECOND EDITION 2000

ISBN 0 906881 07 2

HELMSHORE

Introduction

This book has been compiled to remind people of what Helmshore was like before large-scale development began in the early 1960s. Housing estates, built with scant regard for the essential character of the locality, quickly destroyed the sombre unity that buildings of local millstone grit had provided. At the same time, social habits, influenced in the main by television and the motor car, were changing at a comparable speed with the result that community life, so evident in the pages that follow, was very much diminished.

One would not now expect the entire village to walk in procession as it did in 1911, when George V was crowned; nor are we likely to see again the numerous and varied communal activities that took place outside working hours. Helmshore, as this book shows, was once an active, participating society; and because its members tended to spend their entire lives in the village, they had a strong sense of belonging to the place and a willingness to serve its interests. Inward-looking and narrow-minded many

Helmshore people undoubtedly were and few enjoyed the living standards that are commonplace today; but in spite of these drawbacks, life had much to offer and it is sad to reflect upon what has been lost.

Since the late Derek Pilkington and I compiled the original edition of this book in 1977 change has continued. Helmshore has ceased to be a busy, manufacturing village employing local labour. The power-loom and the spindle are things of the past. Most villagers now work in other places; and many outsiders travel considerable distances to reach their desks at Airtours, by far the district's largest employer.

The book soon went out of print and demand for a new edition grew. In preparing the revised edition of *Helmshore*, John Simpson and I decided to include more than forty old photographs that had been donated to the Local History Society during the previous twenty years. We thank the donors and those people who have helped in other ways to make the book possible.

Chris Aspin

CONTENTS

RAVENSHORE VIADUCT, HELMSHORE

The earliest pictures of Helmshore are two oil paintings of the Ravenshore and Higher Mill Viaducts. They are by an Italian artist and were commissioned by John Torkington (1804 - 1850), the railway contractor who built the line through the village in 1847 - 48. The paintings are now in the Railway Museum, York.

RAVENSHORE to BRIDGE END

Ravenshore at the beginning of the century, when the footpath to Irwell Vale was as popular with villagers as it is today.

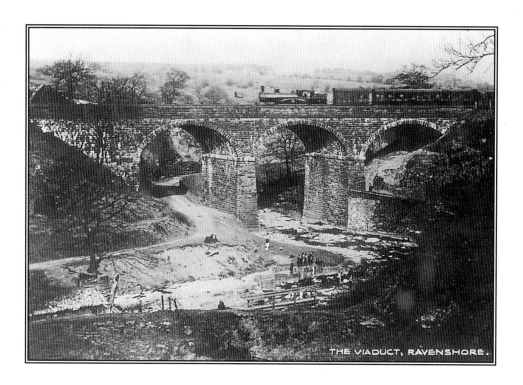

THE VIADUCT, RAVENSHORE.

RAVENSHORE
HELMSHORE

Three views taken from the west side of Ravenshore, often called "Little Blackpool" from the number of bathers who enjoyed themselves in the pools near the viaduct. The photograph on the left shows Ravenshore Cottages and a picnic party on the site of Ravenshore Mill. Above: The derelict mill in 1890. It was originally built in the early 17th century for fulling cloth by water and was rebuilt in 1757.

Snighole in 1905. The settlement grew up alongside two small mills, the ruins of one of which can be seen surrounded by a hedge. The three-storey building was used by hand-loom weavers. Snighole derives its name from "snig" - an eel. Note the woollen cloth stretched on tenter frames at Top o' th' Brow in the upper left-hand side of the picture. This was from Higher Mill. The lower picture shows the now-vanished waterfall, which was built to raise the river level sufficiently to provide water power for Ravenshore Mill. The map was drawn in 1847.

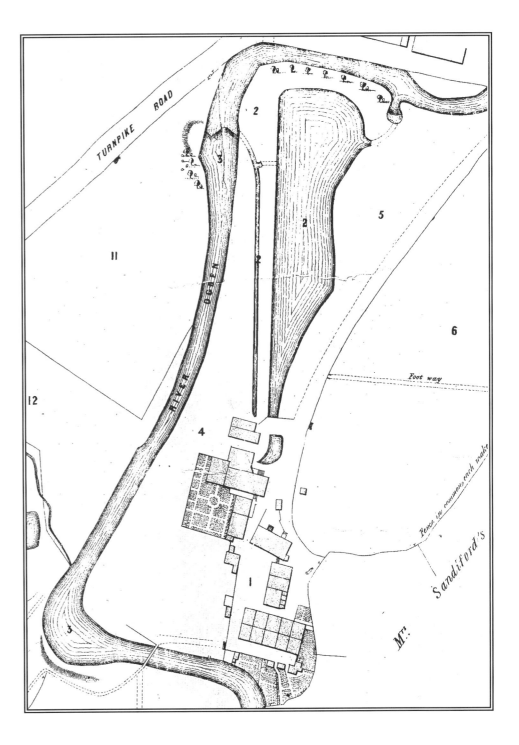

The OPENING of the
Helmshore, Ewood Bridge and
Irwell Vale War Memorial

CLOCK and TOWER

BY

Mrs. W. J. PORRITT,

AND THE

UNVEILING

OF THE

WILLIAM JOHN PORRITT, (Senior)
WILLIAM JOHN PORRITT, (Junior)

AND

HAROLD PORRITT

MEMORIAL
QUADRANT WALL

BY

Mrs. H. PORRITT,

IN THE

"Memorial Grounds," Helmshore,

ON

SATURDAY, 24th JUNE, 1922.

Jas. Pilkington, Printer, Helmshore.

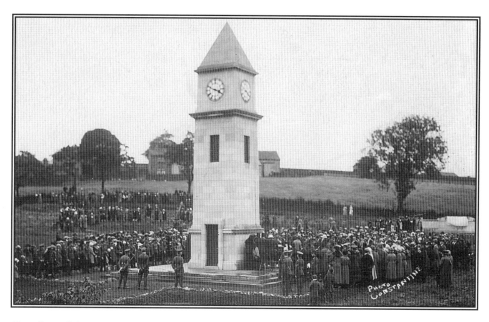

Opening of the Memorial Gardens, which were the gift of the Porritt family. The site was the filled-in reservoir adjoining Snighole Mill. The lower photograph shows Mr. F. W. Malpas, headmaster of the village school, presenting an album to Mrs. W. J. Porritt, who opened the Memorial Tower on which were the names of Servicemen killed during World War I. Mrs. Harold Porritt (seated) later unveiled the Quadrant Wall, (a memorial to her family), which is on the right of the above picture. On the right of the lower picture are Major David Halstead and the two Methodist ministers, Mr. Humble and Mr. Perkins.

Helmshore War Memorial.

To be

Erected to the Memory of the Fifty-two Men of Helmshore, Ewood Bridge, and Irwell Vale, who, at the call of duty, left all they held most dear, endured hardships, and ultimately laid down their lives in the Great War.

The Corner Stones

OF THE

Clock Tower

Will be laid on April 23rd, 1921,

BY

O. W. PORRITT, Esq., J.P.

AND

Mrs. O. W. PORRITT.

Men from the Parish of Musbury who gave their lives in the Service of their Country.

Name	Rank	Regiment	Place	Date
Percy Peacock Law	A.B.	R.N.D.	H.M.S. Hawke, North Sea	Oct. 15, 1914
William Hodson	...	...		Oct. 23, 1914
William Edward Rogers	Pte.	1st R.W.F.	Ypres, Belgium	Nov. 7, 1914
James Henry Mason	Pte.	E.L.	Neuve Chapelle	March 12, 1915
Richard Rawstron	Pte.	K.O.R.L.	France	May 14, 1915
John Wraith Hacking	Pte.	K.S.L.I.	Lockre, France	June 8, 1915
Robert Jackson	Pte.	L.F.	Dardanelles	July 11, 1915
Richard Shaw		G.G.	Hullock, Loos, France	Oct. 4, 1915
Alva Entwistle	Pte.	K.O.R.L.	Ypres, Belgium	March 9, 1916
Richard Entwistle	Pte.	16th Dev.	Moislains, nr. Peronne	Sept. 2, 1918
John William Entwistle	Pte.	K.O.R.L.	Le Havre, France	Aug. 2, 1916
Charles Fulcher	Pte.			
James Ashworth		1st G.G.	France	Sept. 25, 1916
William Harris	Pte.	2nd E.L.	Newport Mil. Hospital	Dec. 29, 1916
William Henry Smith	Pte.	9th E.L.	Darian Balkans	Dec. 27, 1916
Wellington Pilkington	Pte.	8th E.L.	Le Touret Mil. Cem., Maui	Jan 17, 1917
James Lord Kay	Pte.	10th L.F.	Sailly Sailsiels, the Somme	Feb. 10, 1917
Richard Thomas Brown	Pte.	6th E.L.	Gallipoli	Aug. 9, 1915
Thomas Abbott	Pte.	1st. E.L.	Guillemont, the Somme	Oct. 18, 1916
Charles Haworth	Pte.	K.O.R.L.	Amara, Mesopotamia	Apr. 8, 1917
John William Ashworth	Pte.			Apr. 15, 1917
John James Warburton	...	Cheshires	France	June 9, 1917
Barnes Rushton	L-Corp.	K.O.R.L.	France	June 7, 1917
John Richard Rushton	Pte.			
Edward Catterall	Pte.			
John Tattersall		R.A.M.C.	Mil. Hos Squires Gate, Blackpool	July 25, 1917
John Robert Shaw	Pte.	W.G.	Lanemarch, France	July 31, 1917
James Thomas	Pte.	K.O.S.B.	The Somme, France	July 12, 1916
Fred Buck	Pte.	G.G.	France	July 31, 1917
Solomon Hanson	Pte.	1/5 E.L.	Coxyde Military Cemetery Furnes, France	Oct. 19, 1917
Robert Warburton Jackson	Pte.			
Samuel Tomlinson	Corp.	E.L.	Levi Cottage, East Ypres	Oct. 9, 1917
James Arthur Banks	Pte.	K.O.R.L.	Poelcapelle, Belgium	Oct. 10, 1917
Harold Willan	Pte.	L.F.	Somewhere in France	Nov. 16, 1917
Richard James Harper	Corp.	R.A.F.	Somewhere in France	Jan. 8, 1916
John James Hanson	Pte.	L.F.	Wellington Bar. Hos. Bury	March 8, 1918
John Ormerod Nuttall	Pte.	1st G.G.	Bienvilliers Cem., Albert	June 2, 1918
Fred Rawstron	Pte.	E.L.	Ypres	June 12, 1918
Thomas Schofield Beggs	S-Cadet	R.F.C.	Hastings Sanatorium	March 19, 1918
Thomas Entwistle	L-Corp.	R.A.M.C.	Keighley Hospital	March 20, 1918
Edward Rogers	Pte.	8th B.R.	Somewhere in France	April 10, 1918
Herbert Trickett	Pte.	L.F.	Highfield Mil Hos. Liverp'l	April 17, 1918
William Greenhow	Gunner	R.F.A.	Arras Cambrai Rd. France	Aug. 27, 1918
Donald Malpas	Sgt.	R.A.F.	Passhendaele Ridge, Ypres	July 25, 1918
Charles King Harris	Pte.	L.N.L.	Chocques Mil Cem, Bethune	Oct. 1, 1918
Thomas Henry Haworth	A.B.	R.N.V.R.	H.M.S. Otranto Kilchoman, Islay	Oct. 5, 1918
Holden Duckworth	Pte.	R.F.A.		Oct. 8, 1919
Joseph Ludlow	...			
Fred Pollitt	Pte.	Lincolns	Somewhere in France	Oct. 23, 1918
Joseph Robert Adams	Pte.	2nd K.L.	Salonica	Oct. 29, 1917
Thomas Edward Entwistle	Pte.	R.A.M.C.	East Africa	Dec. 15, 1918
John Robert Pilkington	Pte.	E.L.	Gassed at Arras, died at Helmshore	Jan. 4, 1919
Harold Nuttall	Pte.	1/5 E.L.	Pys, France	Aug. 24, 1918
Arthur Crossley	L-Corp.	2nd E.L.	France	Between Mar. 23 & Apr 2, 1918
William Lindsey	Pte.	R.M.L.I.	Arras, France	April 28, 1917
David Rogers	Pte.	1st L.F.	Somewhere in France	July 1, 1916
William Greenwood	Pte.	11th E.L.	The Somme, France	July, 1916
John Thomas Wallwork	Pte.	S.W.B.	Messines Ridge	April 11, 1918
Arthur Heap	Sig.	K.R.R.	The Somme, France	March 21, 1918
James Haworth	Pte.	1/5 E.L.	France	Nov. 6 1918

Bridge End at the turn of the century. The pictures were taken before Private Road was straightened and the barn and shop next to the public house demolished. The shop sold sweets and pies. Directly opposite was a wheelwright's shop, the full extent of which can be seen in the top right-hand photograph. The lower right photograph was taken between 1888 (opening of the Liberal Club) and 1897 (building of Elm Terrace).

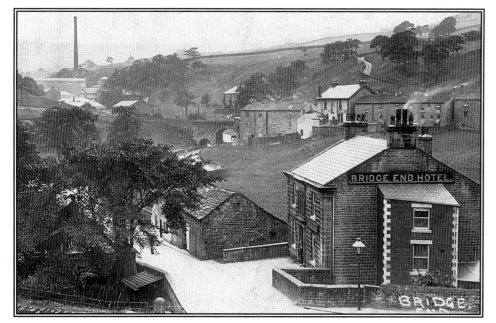

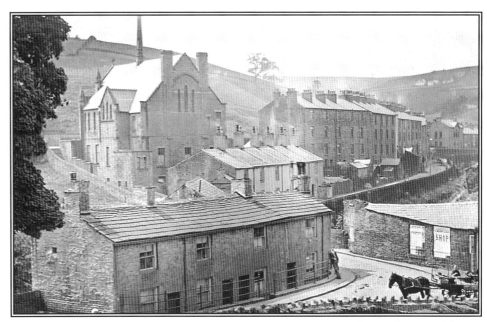

Workers' cottages in the early 19th century were rarely erected on what would now be called good building land. This was considered too valuable and houses were frequently built on hillsides and sometimes, as at Bridge End, on the bed of a river. The row was demolished in 1907 to allow the bridge to be widened.

Hartley Peigh of Haslingden

Lancashire had its pea-wallahs, too, at one time apparently. Of the many itinerant traders once so common in the industrial areas (writes "C. A.") none was more popular than the pea vendor.

A familiar figure in Haslingden during the first quarter of the century was a bearded ancient known as Hartley Peigh, who sold his wares from a converted perambulator of great age. A fire in a bucket heated the peas, while on the sides of the pram was a quaint selection of vinegar bottles and salt sifters. When Hartley toured Helmshore, the village children would sing to the tune of "Colonel Bogey," a little song which began, "Here comes owd Hartley Peigh with his bloomin' char-a-banc," and would answer his cry of "Peighs all hot" with the rejoinder, "Waarm at bottom and cowd at top." My grandfather once placed an old kipper among the peas while Hartley was in a public-house : the results were disastrous and the poor man's reputation was never the same again.

Many photographs in this book were taken by the late Arthur Constantine (left) whose first studio was at Bridge End. It can be seen on the picture taken in 1919 of "Hartley Peigh", who sold hot peas from a perambulator. Note the child with the once-popular iron hoop.

PEACE REJOICINGS.

The year is 1902. The occasion, a procession to mark the end of the Boer War. Both pictures were taken at Bridge End. The cart was decorated by members of the Blue Ribbon Club. Below are four members of the Pilkington family - Luke, Elliot, Rosannah and Robert.

A MIDNIGHT CELEBRATION AT HELMSHORE.

Helmshore, though an outlying portion of the borough of Haslingden, was on the occasion of the declaration of peace much ahead of the town itself. Mr. A. E. Ashworth received about nine o'clock on Sunday night a telegram stating that peace had been declared, but some doubt was felt about the matter. About eleven o'clock, however, there came a confirmatory wire. A few people started to knock up the ringers of Musbury Church and the members of Helmshore Brass Band. By twelve o'clock the fine bells of the church, with their ropes in the hands of one of the best "band" in the country, were ringing out merrily on the otherwise still air. By twenty minutes to two seventeen members of the band had been got together—the remaining members lived too far out to be reached conveniently—and they began to parade the village, playing patriotic and popular airs, such as "See the conquering hero comes," "Hero of Trafalgar," and "God save the King." They called at the different residences of local gentlemen. The ringers left the belfry about half-past two and threw in their lot with the brass band (who illuminated their path with two acetyline lamps mounted on poles), and the heralders of the glad tidings were also joined by a number of other villagers. The triumphant tour of the village was brought to a close at half-past four, and almost all who composed the parade turned out to work at six o'clock the same morning. Most of the workpeople had holiday on Monday afternoon. At Middle Mill so few of the hands returned to work after dinner that the mill could not well be run, and the whole of the machinery was allowed to stop. One mill found it impossible to stop owing to pressure of orders, but the others stopped by consent of those in authority. Banners were put out. In Co-op.-row (or what is known as "Grand Stand") every house flew a colour from its window. On Monday night there was another parade, composed of the brass band; a band got up by the Blue Ribbon Club and provided with mouth-organs, and pans and tins for drums; and 400 to 500 people. The procession was headed by "John Bull," typified by Mr. Wm. McWilton, who is so naturally adapted to this personification that, with suitable get up, he has carried off about six prizes in it. In the rear were a number of people in character. The procession started off at 7-30 and went through the village, the band playing "Where are the boys of the old brigade?" "Valiant Volunteers," "Hero of Trafalgar," "Soldiers of the King," and national airs. As a finale, the processionists grouped together and sang "God save the King," the band accompanying. The front of the residence of Mr. R. V. S. Haughton was illuminated with Chinese lanterns for the occasion.

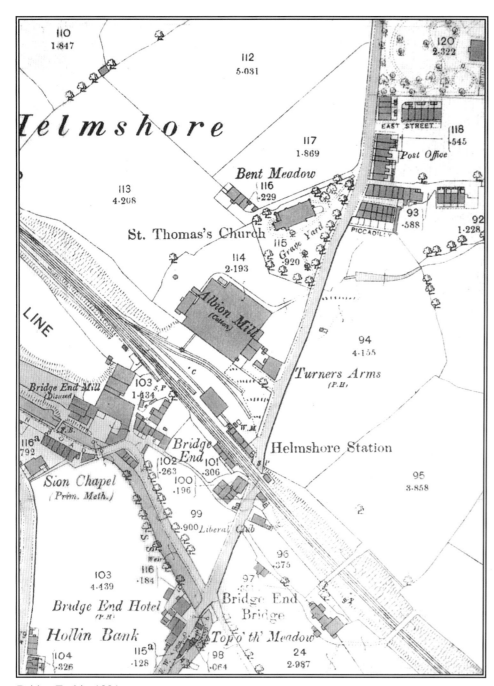

Bridge End in 1891.

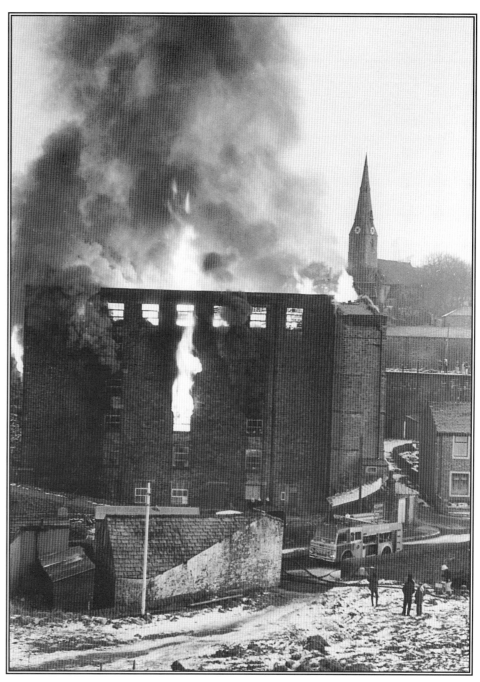

The end of a village landmark. Bridge End Mill fire, January 15, 1982

Workers at Bridge End Mill in 1877. This is one of the first photographs taken in the village. The part of the mill on the left was burned down in April 1885. The fourth girl from the left is Jane Alice Barlow, who was born in 1867. Her great-grandfather built and ran the original Sunnybank Mill in Alden.

Bridge End Mill was used for many years as a wool store by Porritts and Spencer. The top floor, which was linked to a private siding alongside the railway station, was used for wool sorting. The carter is Fred Entwistle, who was about to take his load of wool to Sunnybank Mill. The picture was taken in 1920; that of the sorters a few years later.

Bridge End seen from Station Road in 1905. Below, the cottage at Bridge End, the cellar of which was once a lock-up. There is a reference to it as early as 1848. The building was demolished in 1973.

Above: Mr. Tom Hollin's grocer's shop stood below Co-op Row. It later sold clothes. Below: Mr. Thomas Nuttall kept a butcher's shop at 9, Bridge End and also sold meat from a horse-drawn cart. The picture dates from 1910.

HELMSHORE ROAD

HELMSHORE

Laying the foundation stone of the Liberal Club extension, September, 1906.

Helmshore Liberal Club.

Inaugurating an Extension.

The corner stone of an extension to Helmshore Liberal Club was laid on Saturday afternoon by Mr. Harold Porritt, president of the club. The extension is to cost £820. Towards this about £620 has been raised during the past twelve months, the Porritt family having assisted substantially in this result. At last Saturday's ceremony Mr. H. W. Porritt contributed a cheque for £50 and a collection realised £8 7s.—both of which amounts go to increase the £620 in hand or promised previous to then. Messrs. Mould and Porritt, of Bury, are the architects.

Councillor Walmsley presided over the corner stone laying, and was supported by Mr. H. Porritt, Councillors Shaw and Law, Mr. A. Smethurst, J.P., Mr. S. Pilling, Mr. John Lord, Mr. James Ramsbottom, the Rev. J. Phillipson, and Mr. Jerry Lord (secretary).

The Chairman said that day's ceremony furnished further evidence of the progress that was the motto of the Helmshore Liberal Club. If they had only a little more progress from some of their representatives at Haslingden, they would get more benefit and improvement for the inhabitants generally. They congratulated Mr. O. W. Porritt, the son of their president, upon his appointment as a county magistrate along with the four gentlemen in the Haslingden district who had received similar honour. All five would reflect credit on the borough. Mr. O. W. Porritt was a worthy son of a worthy sire, and if he kept up the family traditions Helmshore Liberalism would have no cause for disappointment, and they wanted men like him, of level-headed intelligence.

By the generosity of the Porritt family (the Chairman continued) the handsome bowling green had been given to the club. This had meant an increase in members, with the result that twelve months ago they had to meet together to consider extension. The result had proved there to be still life and generosity amongst the Liberals of the district. In twelve months they had raised £620, and there was not a club in all Rossendale division that could have done so much with the same number of members. The club was conducted on strict temperance principles, and there was no gambling. No temperance or social club could be conducted on more strict lines for the benefit of the people. The club was useful as a meeting for their members and their municipal representatives. Attendance at Town Council meetings and committees entailed hard labour, but they had the advantage of meeting their constituents and getting to know what they required. The club was also useful for supporting their member and the Government now in power. Legislation was needed for the benefit of the working classes, who wanted such measures as one man one vote, peace, retrenchment and reform, and the revision of the Land Laws, whereby a tenant could be compensated for his improvements.

Methodist Whitsuntide processions at Elm Terrace and the "Field Day", 1927.

Below: Elm Terrace in 1909.

Mr. Rostron Lord (in the straw hat) sold newspapers, stationery and sweets from the wooden hut in Station Brow. The above picture was taken in 1906, shortly after the business began. Many local views reproduced elsewhere in this book are on sale. Mrs. Lord and Miss Annie Lord are in the slightly later photograph. A poster in the window advertises a trip to Northern Ireland for £2 17s 6d. On the right is the village midwife Mrs. Nanny Lord, mother of Rostron.

Bridge End House, the rear of which is at the right of the smaller picture, was added in the 1860s. It later became Nos. 1 and 3 Station Hill and can also be seen in the photograph of the Musbury Whitsuntide procession on page 21. The Manchester and Liverpool District Bank opened a branch there in 1913, and later Mr Fred Mead ran a village store. The photograph on the left shows Sarah Hardman at the door of 11 Station Hill, which overlooked the rear of Elm Terrace. The coalplaces for the houses were in Helmshore Road, facing the Liberal Club (now Sunnybank Social Club). They are shown in the picture above.

Until their demolition in 1972, nine houses occupied the open space below the site of Helmshore railway station. A farm once stood there; but adjoining land was taken for both the turnpike (Helmshore Road) and the East Lancashire Railway. In 1838, the local woollen firm of W. & R. Turner bought the estate and turned the farm buildings into workers' homes.

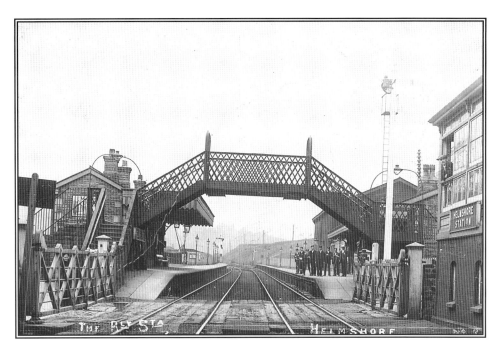

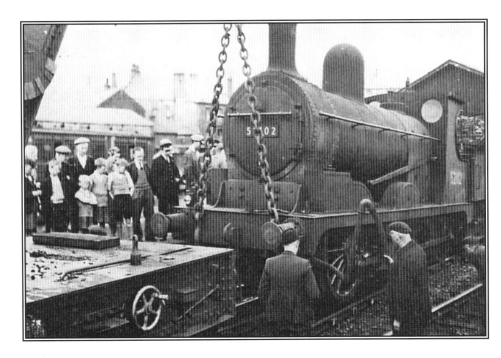

Helmshore station, then part of the Lancashire and Yorkshire Railway Co.'s network, in about 1906. The footbridge was built in 1902. The derailment of the 0-6-0 freight locomotive occurred in the station in 1947.

Helmshore Road in the days when traffic was exceedingly light and processions filled it completely. Top left: Musbury Church Whitsuntide walk in 1908. Below left: Helmshore Band leading a Whitsuntide procession in 1909. Note the advertisement for the Cinema de Luxe at Haslingden with its "animated pictures".

The clock on the lamp standard near the Station Hotel was for the first bus service. The other pictures are of Church Brow. The procession was that of 1911 to mark the Coronation of George V.

Piccadilly shortly before its demolition in 1961. The photograph was taken from Fairhill and also shows part of St. Thomas Street, one side of which was back-to-back with Piccadilly. The settlement began as a farm called Bottom of Flaxmoss. The woollen manufacturers, W. & R. Turner, built the houses in the early 19th century.

Below left: Helmshore Post Office (488 Helmshore Road) in 1935. It had opened, along with the telephone kiosk, in 1928, and continued there until 1998.

Below right: Helmshore Co-operative Society opened its first (and only) branch shop opposite Musbury Church in 1916. The photograph was taken in about 1924.

In the early part of the century, Helmshore Post Office adjoined the Station Hotel. The picture far left shows it in 1911, when it was decorated for the Coronation of George V. The postmaster was Mr. James Pilkington, who was also a printer and stationer. Above right: Mr. Albert Bentley, postman and sign painter, in 1909. He lived in Ivy Cottage, which can be seen on the left. Above left, is Miss Annetta Pilkington, who was a postwoman in the village during World War I.

Helmshore Post Office at No. 452, Helmshore Road, taken about 1890, when it was run by the Misses Barnes.

Musbury Church in about 1875. The clergyman is the Rev. William Sutcliffe, vicar from 1871 to 1882. The photograph pre-dates by several years the building of the lych-gate and enlargement of the churchyard, both of which took place in 1890. The lane was originally part of the main road through the village and continued to Bridge End Mill until the coming of the railway in 1848. The section to Bent Meadow Farm was incorporated into the churchyard and a new lane built at a cost of £150.

MUSBURY CHURCH BELLS

(Contributed by Mr. J. H. Banks, Leader of the Bellringers).

∘∘∘○❸○∘∘∘

As the senior ringer I have been asked to write a short account of our Bells and Ringers. The Bells are a light peal of eight from the foundry of C. and G. Mears (now Mears and Stambank, Whitechapel, London). The tenor, or heaviest bell, is about 10 cwt., and the complete peal is a fine one with the tone extremely good for bells of this weight. We owe the Bells to the generosity of Mr. William Turner, who named each of the first seven bells after his own daughters.

The following are the inscriptions on the bells:—
Treble 1 C. and G. Mears, 1851 Founders, Lond. Wilhelmena.
No. 2 C. and G. Mears, 1851. Margaret Alice.
No. 3 C. and G. Mears, 1851. Eliza.
No. 4 C. and G. Mears, 1851. Adelaide.
No. 5 C. and G. Mears, 1851. Martha.
No. 6 C. and G. Mears, 1851. Helen.
No. 7 C. and G. Mears, 1851. Mary Ann.
Tenor 8 C. and G. Mears, 1851.

> " This peal of eight bells was presented to the new Parish of Musbury by William Turner, Esquire, J.P., and Mrs. Turner, of Flaxmoss House, June 21st, 1851; this bell in their own names, and seven in the names of their respective Daughters as inscribed.',

It will be seen from the above that the date of the Bells was 1851. They were in oak frames and did good service without any considerable repairs until 1912, when Taylor's, of Loughborough Foundry, overhauled and refitted them in an iron frame.

The Bells go wonderfully well, and are considered by all visitors who ring them to be an easy running peal. I can truthfully add that they are well looked after, and their condition now is exceedingly good. The inside of the Tower requires some beautifying, but probably this will be improved in the near future.

To give a short history of the ringers is not, however, as simple as it looks. Bellringers have a language and vocabulary of their own, and any expressions ringers use in Method ringing are entirely lost to the lay public. However, learning to ring bells properly is a strenuous and protracted hobby, and requires a fair degree of perseverance and mathematical ability. There must be no lapse of memory; and even with the above qualities, if they have no musical sense of time and compass, their other qualities are useless. A ringer's motto should be: " How sad sweet music is when time is broke, and no proportion kept."

The bells of Musbury Church have always been much admired and over the years many able teams of ringers have occupied the belfry. The above picture was taken on Jubilee Day, May 6, 1935. The ringers are: Back Row: Thomas Wallwork, Joseph Woods, Thomas Isherwood, James Corbridge, John Wise. Front: Thomas Brandwood, James H. Banks (leader), James Jackson, Bertram Grimshaw.

The Bishop of Blackburn, Dr. P. M. Herbert, visiting Musbury Church in 1927. With him is the vicar, the Rev. A. Winfield. Below: The choir on the church steps in 1900. Right: The Church and lych-gate, 1920.

Helmshore Road in the early days of the century. The photograph of the Sion procession at East Street in 1908 includes many interesting details - the houses and barn at Gregory Fold, the woman with the shawl, two fine perambulators and the posters advertising the "Sermons" at the Wesleyan Chapel. The photograph above was taken in about 1908. Just beyond St. Thomas Street and Piccadilly and on the site of the former co-operative store is an undertaker's workshop run by Eleazar Law. Left: Haymaking in what is now the School Field.

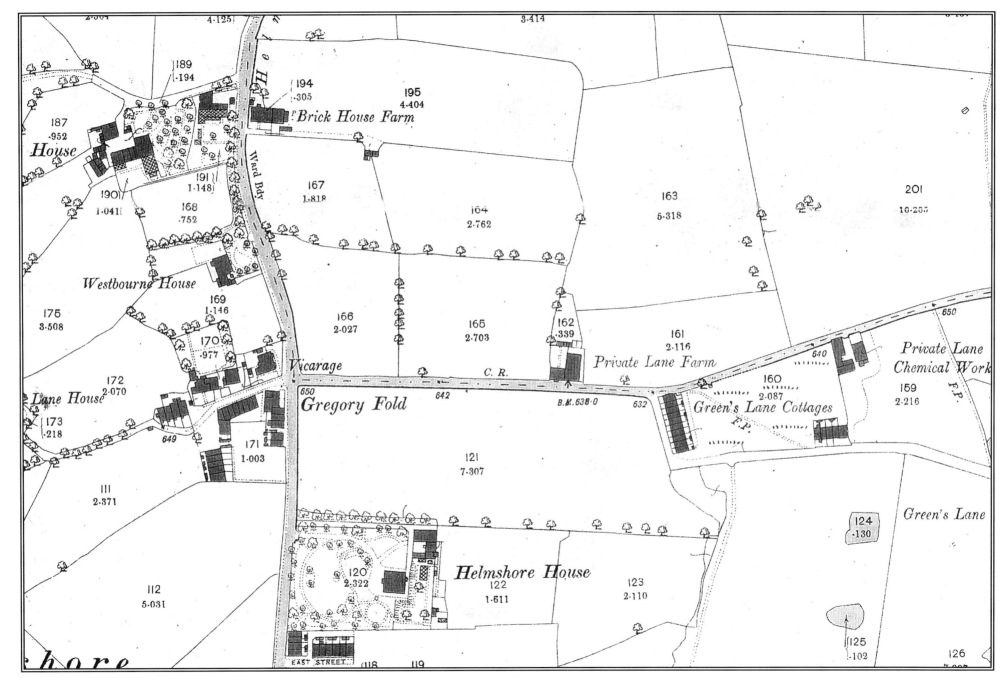

Helmshore in 1891

Gregory Fold. The Methodist Whitsuntide procession always stopped there for hymn singing. The photograph above was taken in 1914 and that on the right in 1947. The choirmaster is Mr. Ben Fisher. The musicians are Mr. Oliver Pilkington (clarinet) and Mr. Jim Ashworth and Mr. Tom Fitton (violins). Guide House, at the corner of Gregory Fold Lane, was demolished shortly after the picture was taken.

The Haslingden Carnival Procession of 1951 is seen at the junction of Helmshore Road and Broadway. Z Men were Army reservists, then in the news because of the Korean War. The picture shows the row of 1820 houses which were soon to come down.

The Council School at Gregory Fold replaced the old National School in 1908 and was officially opened on June 2, 1909 by Alderman T. B. Hamilton, Mayor of Haslingden. Pictured above right is the first infants' class at the new school. Right: a drill lesson for Miss Brierley's class in the schoolyard in the early 1930s. Above is the view one had in those days from the school window. The farmer is Jeffrey Willan, who also represented Helmshore Ward on Haslingden Council. The photograph was taken in 1940.

Some of the hundreds of children who have attended the school. The top left picture was taken in 1927 when Mr. J. W. Holgate was headmaster; that below left in 1947. The master is Mr. John Jenkinson, who succeeded Mr. Holgate. Above: Miss Pilling taught at the school from 1923 to 1962. She is pictured with her class in 1955. Below: Miss Rimington's class playing games on the school field in the same year.

William Turner (1793 - 1852) influenced the development of Helmshore more than any other person. He joined the family woollen business as a young man and greatly extended it. Turner lived at Flaxmoss House within easy reach of his four mills - Higher, Middle (now Airtours), Tanpits and Bridge End. The business was one of the largest in the woollen trade and exported to many parts of the world. Most of the 2,000 workpeople lived in the firm's houses in Helmshore. A few of these (notably Spring Gardens) are still used. Turner was largely responsible for the building of the railway through the village and it was he who laid the foundation stone of the Higher Mill Viaduct in June 1847. Turner married twice and had eleven daughters. On his death, the mills closed, causing hundreds of people to leave the village. It took a century for the population of Helmshore to climb back to that of 1852.

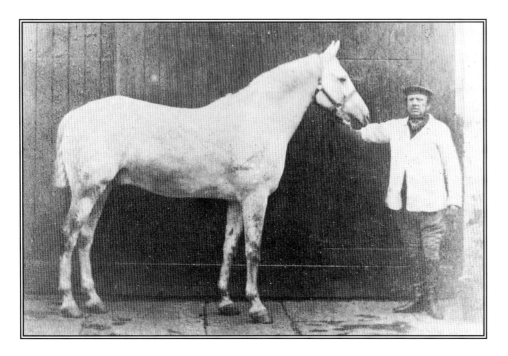

These photographs were taken in about 1880 at Flaxmoss House, then owned by George Ashworth Smith. His groom, William McWilton, is in both photographs. He was known as John Bull Senr., for like his son, William McWilton, he often took the part in carnivals and processions.

On the left of the upper picture is Chris ("Kester") Willan, who came from Yorkshire to Helmshore to be cowman for a previous owner of Flaxmoss House, William Turner, the woollen manufacturer. The servants pose with the implements of their trades, including a manure basket, a two-prong rake and a long spade for mole-catching.

Flaxmoss House in 1904. It had been rebuilt in the early 1890s by George Ashworth Smith (above right), and in 1894 became the first house in the village to be lit by electric light. The sale notice dates from 1919.

The picture on the right shows Brick House Farm, which stood opposite Flaxmoss House in Helmshore Road. It took its name from a nearby brick kiln. The farm and its "twin" at Helmcroft (facing Turfcote) were built by the Smith family for people who worked for them. The story goes that both buildings were made single-storey to prevent servants looking into the grounds of their masters' mansions.

The Helmshore end of Broadway in 1933. Turning the old Dow Lane into a wide new road began on April 1, 1930, under a Government scheme to help the unemployed. The old lane was widened and straightened between Gregory Fold and Pilkington Terrace, from which point a new section went to Manchester Road. Broadway was completed by the end of 1931 and officially named in January of the following year.

A winter's day in the 1890s. The shop of John Scott Pickup in Helmshore Road was a village landmark for many years. Mr. Pickup, a leading Primitive Methodist, was a Liberal councillor for Helmshore for nine years and served on the Board of Guardians for eighteen years. He died in 1922, aged 67. Mr. Pickup's father kept a grocer's shop in the third house from the left from 1853 until his death some thirty years later. J. S. Pickup then built the shop in the photograph.

Before Broadway was built in the early 1930s, Helmshore was linked to Bentgate by Private Lane, better known as Dow Lane. Close to the junction of Lancaster Avenue was the stone-built Private Lane Farm, pictured above with members of the Walsh family, who farmed the surrounding land for many years. Further along the lane and just short of the High School grounds was the soap works of William Hoyle and Sons. There had previously been a brick kiln on the site. The firm issued the poster in praise of carbolic soap in August 1894.

19

TO THE PUBLIC OF HASLINGDEN & NEIGHBOURHOOD.

Owing to the OUTBREAK OF SMALL-POX,

WILLIAM HOYLE & SONS,

SOAP AND CHEMICAL MANUFACTURERS, HASLINGDEN,

Take the opportunity of informing the Public generally, that they are Manufacturers of a PURE, SPECIAL

CARBOLIC SOAP

Made from the Finest Materials and guaranteed free from any adulteration.   It possesses both strong Disinfecting and Cleansing Properties.

No Family should be without it, as it tends to

STOP THE SPREAD OF ALL INFECTIOUS DISEASES.

Carbolic Acid is considered by all medical and scientific men to be the most powerful disinfecting agent known, and this Soap contains a very large percentage of that agent.

Use it FOR THE TOILET AND WASHING YOUR LINEN, as disease germs cannot live in its presence.

Ask your Grocer for it, and see you get it.

Yours most respectfully,

BEWARE OF IMITATIONS.   **WM. HOYLE & SONS.**

J. J. RILEY, Printer, "Free Press" Office, Rawtenstall.

Houses now cover the field at New Barn (left) and Higher Cockham Farm, built in 1778, disappeared when the golf course was extended in the early 1970s. The photograph of the Greens Lane cottages was taken at the beginning of the century. The third from the left was once the Robin Hood beerhouse.

Two photographs of Lane Head Farm, now incorporated into the Golf House. They were taken in about 1904, the year the Rossendale Golf Club was founded. Greens Lane Farm, the subject of the verses, was invariably known as the Boggart House. It was built by the side of the lane on a site opposite the present High School. Sightings of a phantom horse have been claimed in fairly recent times.

LINES ON GREEN LANE BOGGERT.

IF we know a man, whose head is white with age and hoary,
How we love to hear him tell a good old timeworn story,
Of dark and wild, and weird romance,
Which moves the heart and makes it dance.

Some strange adventure which he saw or knew when quite a lad,
And as he tells the story, it makes his heart feel sad ;
But now the storys finished, then comes what pleases most,
He finishes the evening with the story of a Ghost.

He tells a flying Phantom, which flys from east to west,
Of lanes and haunted houses, and woods among the rest,
and speaks of white-robed figures, which appear in the dark,
But mostly ends the story, by saying 'twas done for a lark.

But the Ghost of which I wish to speak, it comes not for a lark,
But mostly when the Phantom comes, it is evening after dark.
It comes, and will not be delayed, by either door or lock,
And the time when it appears, they say, is night at 12 o'clock.

I do not wish to argue now, 'twould only waste my time,
But I'll try to tell my story in plain and simple rhyme ;
Well, the Boggert that is causing the folks so much alarm,
Has taken up its residence at a place called Green Lane Farm.

It's half-a-mile from Woolpack, perhaps a little more,
Perchance a little further away from Helmshore ;
However, distance matters not in what I'm going to tell,
Suffice it for the present, it's a place you all know well.

They say it comes in various forms, you may think my words
        are wild,
And yet they say it sometimes comes in the form of a beautiful
        child,
With bright blue eyes and curly hair, and rosy cheeks as well,
But from whence it comes and whither it goes, my friends I
        cannot tell.

There's the form of a dog in which it is seen, and the form of
        a woman's mother,
She comes and she looks with dazzling eyes, let's hope it's
        the young child's mother,
Searching for her long lost child—If so, let's hope she'll find,
To possess her child so beautiful, will ease her motherly mind.

They say it assumes the form of a man, it sounds very strange,
        yes rather,
We can but hope, as we hope'd before, that now it's the young
        child's father,
They say it comes in at the door, like children's skip and hop,
Straight through the house and then upstairs and out at the
        chimney top.

Besides being seen, it's to be heard to sound like rustling silk,
And one has asked the question, does the Boggert ere give
To tell his name, I dare not, it's not my privelege,   [milk.
But the man that ask'd the question, he lives at Ewood Bridge.

It's, if you want to know, well that I cannot tell,
But some folks say, for ages past, it at Green Lane Farm did
        dwell,
One day the farmer thought ne'd try to make this Phantom
        shift,
And not being strong enough himself, he thought he'd get a
        lift.

I don't know the name of the man who came, whether Jack
        or Bob,
But sufficient for the present, he undertook the job,
They say he talks with spirits and they think him one of their
        best,
And he gives it in his verdict, that a spirit cannot rest.

He tells the farmer and his wife, that what he says he'll prove,
So without expense he'll undertake to make this spirit move,
He very likely tried himself to move it without bother,
However he couldn't manage it, so he had to ask another.

So now these spiritualists tried their hands,
To see if they could move it from its ancient stand,
And some folks say, though to me its odd,
They got it away as far as God.

But from its ancient haunt, this spirit would not sever,
For soon it landed back and became as busy as ever,
And these spiritualistic men ever since that day,
From the place called Green Lane Farm, they mind to keep
        away.

One night some friends, just after dark,
With boggert, thought they'd have a lark,
And the farmer joining in the fun,
He loaded his double-barrelled gun.

And they agreed if it came to a certain spot,
That one of the party should have a shot,
So they sat down and waited till the time it should come,
They were determined to see it, before they went home.

They had not waited long, when it came with a roar,
So they jumped on their feet, and made for the door,
With the hair on their heads, it were standing like wire,
And the gun in their hands, were determined to fire.

But it all came to nought, for no ghost could they see,
And the one with the gun, how simple looked he,
And there hasn't been one of them, e'er heard to boast,
Or tell what he thought about shooting the ghost.

Now its pretty well known in all nature's laws,
That there's ne'er an effect, without there's a cause,
And as this effect, is plain for to see,
The thing that has made it must somewhere be.

So two or three chaps, o'er to Green Lane went,
To discover this cause, where their intent,
And to search in the cellar, they all agreed,
If the farmer would find them, all they would need.

So they got a good dinner, to act as propeller,
Then they marched to their work, down into the cellar,
Then into the bottom, like an unringed pig,
With a pick and a spade they began to dig.

They found plenty of dirt, and gravel and stones,
But alas ! they could find no human bone,
And for fear that the bones in the dirt might be lurked,
With their hands they every spadeful searched.

As the digging proceeded each other they chaffed,
While up in the house the farmer he laughed,
Like miners they dug for nearly a yard,
But no bones could they find to act as reward.

But at last they gave up, and with common consent
They picked up their tools, and up steps they went,
And the farmer he chuckled and laughed in good glee,
As he chaffed these hard workers, while having their tea.

And what did they think ? well, one of them owns
That he'll ne'er go again a hunting for bones ;
And what were their names ? I'm not going to tell,
Sufficient for me they did their work well.

Now before I conclude, I just wish to state,
That the persons who have seen it, they live at Bent Gate :
And they toffy, and pies, and Eccles Cakes sell,
But the names of the persons I don't wish to tell.

And now, ye men who with spirits out,
Never try again this Ghost to steal,
For if you manage to get it away,
It is sure to be back again next day.

And ye that searched for human bones,
Amongst the gravel and the stones,
Now don't be vexed or take offence,
If I hope in the future you will learn more sense.

And you men who of your bravery boast,
Just go and try to catch this Ghost ;
And if you think it will mend the fun,
Just try and shoot it with a gun.

                                H.—(Copyright.)

The day Helmshore was cut off. The snowfall in January 1940 was the heaviest recorded. Road and rail traffic was disrupted for several days until drifts like that shown blocking Helmshore Road at Turfcote were cleared. The lower left picture shows the road on a sunny day. Helmcroft cottages, now demolished, were built in 1763; the stone bungalow in 1895. The view below is of Helmshore Road in the early 1920s.

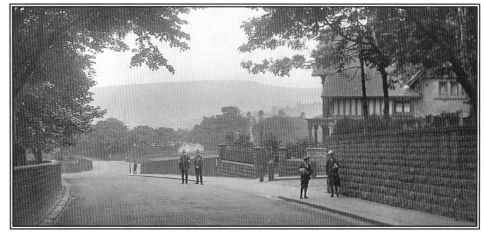

ALDEN and MUSBURY

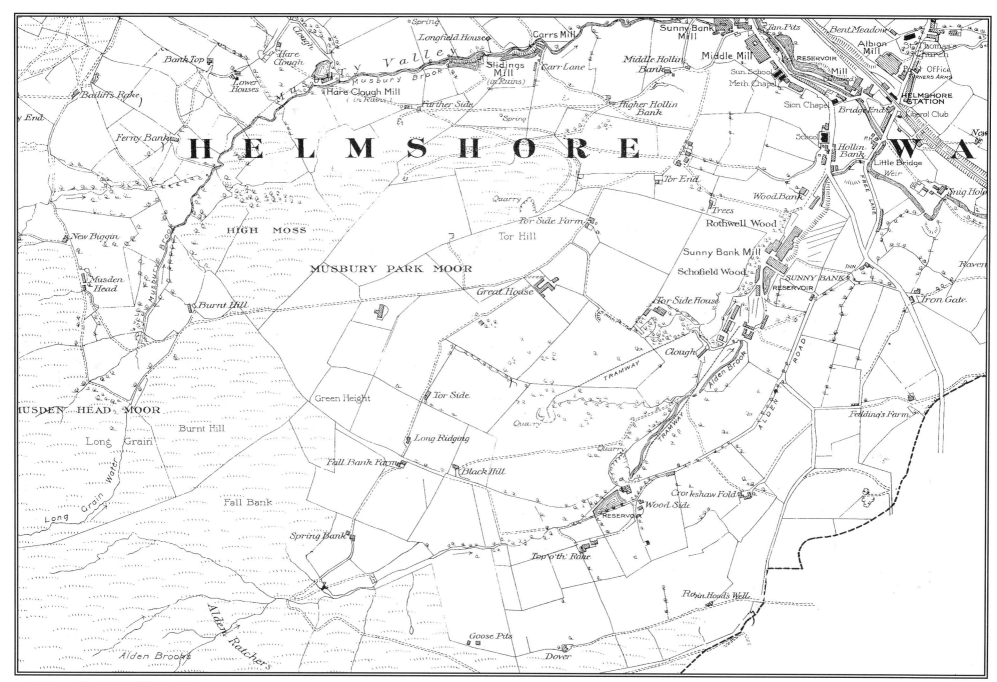

ALDEN AND MUSBURY IN 1901

Above left: Tor Side in 1910. Tor Side House in the centre of the picture was built by Mr. W. J. Porritt in the late 1860s.

Left: Alden Road at the beginning of the century. The quarry at the end of the lane was then in use. One of the cranes is just visible.

Above: Robin Hood's Well on the old road between Haslingden and Bolton.

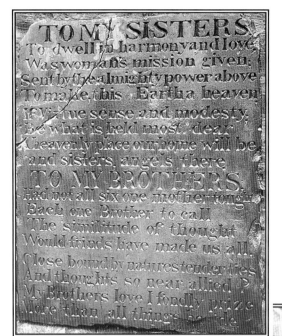

TO MY SISTERS

To dwell in harmony and love
Was woman's mission given
Sent by the almighty power above
To make this Earth a heaven.
If Virtue sense and modesty
Be what is held most dear
A heavenly place our home will be
and sisters, angels there.

TO MY BROTHERS

Had not all six one mother tought
Each one Brother to call
The similitude of thought
Would frinds have made us all.
Close bound by natures tender ties
And thoughts so near allied.
My Brothers love I fondly prize
More than all things beside.

The Pilkington family is one of the oldest in Helmshore. Robert ("Rough Robin") settled in Alden, the upper part of which is still known as the Township of Pilkington. He acquired his nickname because he invariably referred to the weather as being "a bit rough". He enclosed common land on the adjoining moor, but would not pay his rates. He was therefore refused relief during the depression of 1826, but appealed to the government for redress, saying he lived at the Township of Pilkington. The name stuck and Robert was dubbed the Marquis of Pilkington. As well as farming, he built a bleach works at the head of the valley close to Spring Bank Farm, pictured above. Several members of the family were skilled stonemasons. James (right) carved the stone above, copying the words from a letter sent by a brother who had emigrated to America. For many years the stone stood outside Spring Bank Farm. The picture of James Pilkington was taken at Holcombe, when he was building Douglas Street. Though illiterate, he carved many gravestones, relying on his son Thomas for guidance. He also carved the inscriptions on the Pilgrims' Cross monument, erected on Holcombe Moor in 1902. (See next page). Working on the bleak moor is said to have hastened his death.

The illustration on the left is of the souvenir plate depicting the memorial.

On the moor between Helmshore and Holcombe, at an altitude of 1,209 feet, is the monument to Pilgrims' Cross. It marks the site of an earlier stone, which was destroyed by vandals in 1901. The origin of this stone is unknown, but it was probably the base of a marker stump on an ancient track. It is popularly believed that the name derives from the fact that pilgrims crossed the moor on their way to Whalley Abbey, but there is a reference to the cross in 1176, more than a century before the abbey was built. At the instigation of the Rev. H. Dowsett, vicar of Holcombe, a memorial was set up in 1902 on the site of the old cross. This consists of a massive block, 5 ft high and 3 ft square, set on a base stone 4½ feet square and a foot thick. The stones were quarried at Fletcher Bank, Shuttleworth and, as the above picture taken on May 24, 1902, shows, were taken by a team of 12 horses onto the moor. Together the stones weigh five tons.

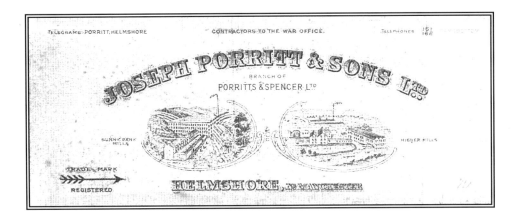

The Porritt Family

Joseph Porritt

William John Porritt

For just over a century, Sunnybank Mill (left) at the entrance to the Alden Valley was the principal place of work for Helmshore people. There had been small water-powered mills on the site before 1866, when Joseph Porritt began his woollen business, but they never expanded. Porritt transformed the area, extending his mill both outwards and upwards until it stretched from one slope of the valley to the other. Because the valley was V-shaped the top floor was longer than the bottom one and it was on this high level that the world's widest woollen looms were later installed. The photograph was taken in 1900, before the extensions were complete.

Joseph Porritt and Sons specialised in papermakers' felts and under the founder's dedicated guidance became within a short time the world's leading supplier. Before the turn of the century the company acquired Higher Mill and Bridge End Mills, supplying the former with electricity generated at Sunnybank. Higher Mill was later sold, but Bridge End continued as the wool depot with a wool-sorting room on the top floor.

William John Porritt, Joseph's elder son, built Tor Side House and acquired most of the land in the valley. From his own quarries there, he provided stone not only for his growing mill and workers' houses, but also for the buildings of St. Annes, of which he was one of the founders.

In 1914, the firm of Porritts and Spencer was formed - the Spencers were Sunnybank employees who set up on their own in Bury in 1904 - and the enlarged group continued to dominate the papermakers' felt trade. The mill was demolished during the 1970s, the chimney being the last to go on Sunday, July 17, 1977 at 5.26 p.m. Porritts and Spencer had merged with the Scapa Group and Sunnybank had no place in the future of the enlarged concern.

Sunnybank from the air. This photograph taken in 1921 shows very well the way in which the mill grew upwards and outwards to fill the valley. Below: An 80 ft. loom installed at the mill during the inter-war years. This and a slightly larger loom were then the widest in the world.

By the turn of the century, Sunnybank Mill was generating its own electricity. The picture above shows Fred and Ben Barker, engineers and electricians, in 1900. The photographs on the right were taken several years earlier and show the blacksmiths' shop and the engine house.

Above: "Mill Bottomers" (men who worked in the bottom room of the mill) in 1900. They were responsible for fulling (that is the shrinking and thickening) of the woven cloth and were required to handle heavy damp pieces.

Below: The felting room staff with their overseer, Mr. Frank Mitchell, in the late 1930s. Their job was to examine the finished felts and rectify any faults.

Right: Workmen digging away the hillside in 1913 to make way for a new cardroom, later weaving shed. The rock was used to fill the reservoir at Snighole, now part of the Memorial Gardens.

Tor Side House in 1911 after extensive alterations by O. W. Porritt. The photograph is one of several he commissioned and displayed in a de luxe album. The right-hand photograph is of the nursery.

As well as helping to run the woollen mills of Porritts & Spencer, Mr. Oliver Porritt farmed in Alden, where he kept a herd of dairy cattle and supplied Helmshore with certified milk. The top photograph shows Fred (left) and Jordan Entwistle harvesting at Great House in the 1920s. The round building was Mr. Porritt's first silo, which was severely damaged by fire on August 25, 1935.

The smaller picture shows farmhands in a ploughed field below Charity Farm during the First World War. The farm, built in 1741, acquired its name in the 19th century. Between 1831 and 1887, it was owned by the trustees of Richard Haworth's Charity, which was established in 1760 to provide relief for the poor of Walmersley-cum-Shuttleworth.

FULLING MILLS
AND
Public House to Let.

TO BE LET,
BY TENDER,

With Possession at the usual times in the Spring of the year 1840.—Firstly.—All that Valuable

FULLING
MILL,

With the Stove and Drying-Houses, Mill-Gearing, Fixed Machinery, Lodge of Water, and other privileges; and also the Dwelling-House and Parcels of Land, containing altogether 5A. 3R. 16P., or thereabouts, in Statute Measure, contiguous thereto, situate near *Midge Hole*, within the Township of Haslingden, in the County of Lancaster, now in the occupation of *Mr. G. Ashworth*, or his undertenants.

AND SECONDLY.—ALL THAT OTHER VALUABLE

Fulling Mill,

With the Stove-House, Mill-Gearing, Fixed Machinery, Lodges of Water, and other privileges; and also the Dwelling-House, formerly used as an Inn, with the several Closes or Parcels of Meadow and Pasture Land, occupied therewith, containing altogether 14A. 3R. 19P., or there-abouts, in the like Measure, situate at *Stake Lane*, within the Township of Haslingden afore-said, now in the occupation of *Edmund Barnes.*

AND THIRDLY.—ALL THAT

INN, OR PUBLIC-HOUSE,

Known by the Sign of the "*White Horse*," also situate at *Stake Lane* aforesaid, and on the side of the Turnpike Road leading from Blackburn through Haslingden Grane to Holcome, also now in the occupation of the said *Edmund Barnes.*

The Mills and Machinery are in a state of excellent repair, and are in every respect calculated for carrying on extensive and profitable business.

Tenders for taking the Premises altogether or separately, stating the amount of Rent, the Term for which the offer is made and other particulars, to be delivered before the 1st of *January,* 1840, at the Office of Mr. ROBINSON, Solicitor, Blackburn, or at CLITHEROE CASTLE, where any further information may be obtained. The present Tenants will show the Premises.

Blackburn, November 13th, 1839.

J. WALKDEN, PRINTER AND STATIONER, KING WILLIAM STREET, BLACKBURN.

Midgehole Mill referred to in the poster was at Woodbank and the cottages in the upper photograph were built from its stones. The picture, which was taken about 1905, shows (top left) the tenter frames on which woollen cloth from the mill was stretched and dried out of doors. The open land on the right was known as The Rock. Boys played football and cricket there until it was enclosed and trees planted. The lower photograph shows the three managers' houses built at Woodbank by the Porritts. It was taken in about 1896.

Musbury Tor. In the 14th century, the hill and its two valleys were enclosed as a deer park by the Earl of Lincoln. Great House and Park House are names that have come down from that period. The park survived for nearly two centuries, but in 1507 it was divided among eight people and developed as farmland.

The photograph above was taken on the top of Tor at 6 a.m. on June 29, 1927, shortly before a total eclipse of the sun. The children are wearing viewers given by the *Haslingden Observer*.

The poem (below) was written by Mr.(later Alderman) J.C. Witham, of Helmshore.

MUSBURY TOR.

Musbury Tor ! that grand old hill,
  Where many a brooklet takes its rise,
Whose frowning rocks of sober grey
  Seem to reach upward to the skies.

And all around its furrowed sides
  The stunted whimberry bushes grow ;
But not a tree or shrub is there,
  To charm the eye or deck its brow.

The outline, table-like and round,
  At once arrests the stranger's eye ;
Its graceful form is soon observed,
  In contrast to the hills close by.

And as you gaze upon its form,
  Though neither tree nor shrub be there,
It has a grandeur of its own,
  A grandeur dignified and rare.

Towering o'er the vale below—
  A fine old rock seen from afar
Stands out majestic and alone ;
  In Musbury 'tis called the knar*.

Some giant hand hath cast it there,
  Its surface poised towards the vale ;
Or some upheaval years ago
  Hath bared it to the passing gale.

On its smooth brow we oft have stood
  To view the neighbouring hills around—
Old Pendle, Criddea, Whittle Pike,
  Coupe-law, and lesser hills abound.

And often have we stood and watched
  The fleecy clouds high overhead
Pass o'er the sun's bright noon-day face,
  And cover the hills with light and shade.

We oft have watched the sun go down,
  And fondly lingered as it sank
With crimson flush and roseate glow
  O'er heathery dell and ferny bank.

There's many a fine old looking hill,
  And many a bold and rocky knor,*
But none like thee we love so well,
  Thou grand old rugged Musbury Tor.

March, 20th, 1883.

    *Knar from the German Knor, a hard knot.

Above left: Longfield House, Musbury, in 1902. It was built about 1800 by the Worsick family, who ran Slidings Mill on the opposite side of the stream. The photograph was taken at a time when the Porritts went grouse shooting on the nearby moor. Their dogs were kept in the kennels next to the house. Below left: Great House Farm, now demolished. The name derived from a building erected on the site soon after the enclosure of Musbury Park at the beginning of the 14th century. The stone above the door is dated 1600, though most of the building probably came later. Above right: Tor from Hare Clough in 1946. The abandoned farms were fast falling into decay. Right: A "dig-it-yourself" coal mine in the clough below Causeway End. The picture was taken during the General Strike in 1926.

Oliver Porritt's first grouse shoot at Causeway End, August 12, 1899. Mr. Porritt (with gun) is in the centre of the group. The boy to his left is Horace Spencer, who later became a director of Porritts & Spencer. He donated the photograph to the Local History Society. Johnny Mort, game keeper, is third from the left (seated). He began his working life at the age of eight in Slidings cotton mill in Musbury. Ike Bumper (Alec Hadcroft), a village "character", is on the extreme right. The gentlemen had potato pies with tomatoes, the rest pies without tomatoes, delivered by cart from Tor Side. The butts were towards Hog Lowe Pike.

Musbury Valley, the favourite beauty spot of most Helmshore people. This picture was taken before the flood of July 1964 destroyed much of the brookside footpath. Above: Sheep ready for dipping near Hare Clough, a photograph taken before World War I. The goat and dog were dipped along with the sheep. Right: Mort's donkey which lived in the valley for many years and is seen here being ridden by Harold Mort. Longfield House is in the background.

Ernest Taylor (left) and Roy Gibbons muckspreading at Kilnfield in May, 1944, after ploughing for the war effort. John Berry, a Musbury farmer with a homespun philosophy, took space in the local paper in 1934 to alert the public to the virtues of bottled milk and new-laid eggs.

HOLCOMBE ROAD

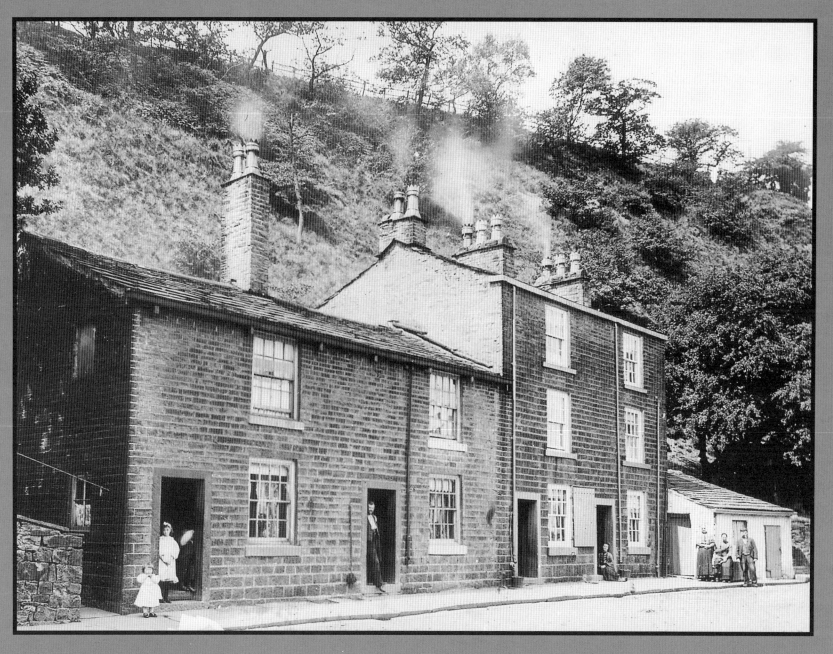

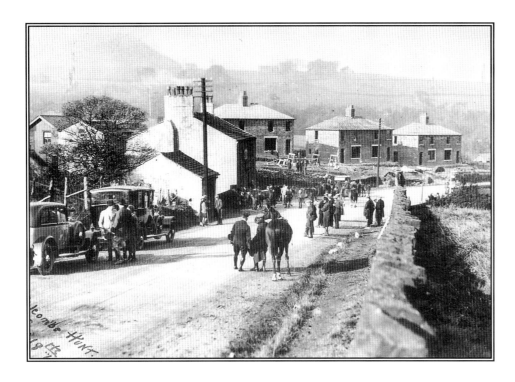

A biplane flying from Glasgow to Manchester made a forced landing near Iron Gate on the evening of January 31, 1933. It struck an electric cable to Richard Rodwell's poultry farm at Kenyon Clough. The pilot and his passenger escaped unhurt. Above: The Holcombe Hunt at the White Horse in November, 1926. Note the Council houses nearing completion. The six were built for a total of £2,970.

Residents in the Ravenshore district of Helmshore had a 'thrill on Wednesday night when an airplane was compelled to make a forced landing owing to shortage of petrol. The machine, which had a passenger besides the pilot, was carrying films from Glasgow to Manchester, and the two men had a narrow escape from electrocution when the machine fouled a Corporation overhead electricity cable and crashed.

The men, who escaped uninjured, were Henry Guy Rivers Malet, of 29, East Fountain Bridge, Edinburgh, the pilot, and Charles Frederick Almond, of the same address. The machine was a Fox Moth, belonging to the Scottish Motor Traction Company, of Edinburgh, for whom Mr. Malet is chief pilot.

The machine left Glasgow at 3-40 p.m. After battling with terrific head winds the occupants discovered that they were running short of petrol and decided to land. This was about 6-20, when they were near Haslingden.

People in different parts of Haslingden and the Bury-road district of Rawtenstall saw the aircraft hovering about with its navigation lights.

Its movements gave the impression that the pilot was endeavouring to get his bearings. Actually he was seeking a landing place. The machine was at this time flying so low that people in their homes could hear the throbbing of the engine and many went outside to look for the plane.

Some people in the Helmshore district said it seemed as though they could have shouted to the pilot and told him where to land. The landing place selected, in fields near Irongate, Helmshore, was good except for the obstructing cable, which was obscured in the darkness.

A BLUE FLASH.

The machine struck it and there was a sudden blue flash which created alarm and caused people to hurry to the place from a wide area. The undercarriage of the machine was badly damaged, and she landed on her nose.

The cable was erected quite recently by Haslingden Corporation for supplying electricity to Kenyon Clough Poultry Farm and Shore Farm, and also to about a quarter of a mile of lane. The breaking of the cable caused consternation at Kenyon Clough. Gas-heated incubators, with an egg capacity, of 10,000, had nine weeks ago been replaced by electrically-heated incubators.

The failure of the current brought risk of heavy loss. Luckily, the gas-heated incubators had been retained temporarily, and the owner of the farm, Mr. Richard Rodwell, and his family and staff set to work to transfer the eggs to them from the electrical machines. They had a big task, working all night, but it was lighter than it might have been because the previous day 936 chickens were hatched and sent away.

The Haslingden Corporation have agreed to fix up a temporary supply to Mr. Rodwell's poultry farm.

STAYED AT THE QUEEN'S, RAWTENSTALL.

Later in the evening the two airmen, after they had done what was possible in regard to their machine and the freightages they were conveying, proceeded to the Queen's Arms Hotel, Rawtenstall, and booked rooms. They seemed little the worse for their alarming experience.

Mr. Malet remained until Thursday and his companion left yesterday.

Hollin Bank at the beginning of the century. The Wesleyan and Musbury processions show villagers in their Sunday best. Helmshore Band, taken on Coronation Day, 1911, has just passed the old toll bar on the right (now demolished).

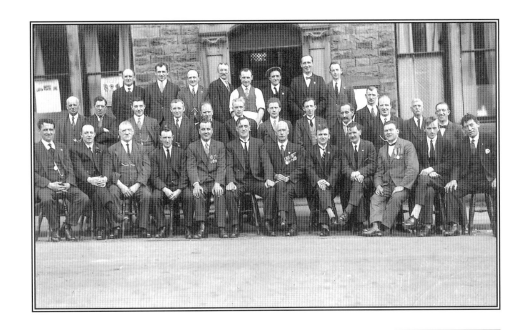

HELMSHORE.

The British Legion Club (in this 1930s photograph of Holcombe Road) replaced the Mechanics' Arms, which had closed in 1926. The new club received a drinks licence despite strong objections from the village churches. Top left: Members and guests at the opening of the club in June, 1927. Left: The programme for the village Old Folk's Treat, which the British Legion Club sponsored in 1928.

The National School was also St. Thomas' Sunday School. The top photograph shows some of the scholars who took part in the Coronation procession of 1902; that below the Church Lads' Brigade in 1916. The vicar is Mr. Winfield.

From the school log books

June, 1866   (Headmaster Mr. Miles Knowles): This morning I had open rebellion in the school. William Pilkington came dirty to school. Refused to answer my questions and on punishing him, used impudent language. Tied him to the pillar which brought him back to his senses, whereupon he answered respectfully all my questions and promised not to offend again.

February, 1877   (Headmaster Mr. James Lister): A "buck" was knocked from the street against one of the window panes with some force, but fortunately did not break it. I went out at once and took all the "bucks", and on returning them this afternoon, cautioned the owners of them and all present against playing the game in such dangerous proximity to the school.

February, 1882   Several boys late: been running after hounds. Kept them behind until 5 o'clock for extra lessons.

May 17, 1900   (Headmaster Mr. William Malpas): A party of boys, numbering 25 to 30, arrived at the school at 2.30 p.m. after registers had been closed. They gave their excuse that Mafeking had been relieved and that they had been for a march to Haslingden to celebrate the event.

Children from the National School at Hollin Bank. The upper photograph was taken in 1901. Mr. Malpas, the headmaster, is on the right. The other picture is of children posing on the footpath opposite the school in 1894. The tall boy at the back is Roland Spencer, who, with his brother Horace (seated centre) were to become directors of Porritts and Spencer. Their father, J. H. Spencer, set up his own woollen business in Bury in 1904. This merged with the Porritt mills in 1914. Some of the children have borrowed adult clothing for the occasion.

AMATEUR DRAMA AT HELMSHORE.

CHURCH SOCIETY IN A FARCE.

Musbury Church Sunday School Dramatic and Choral Society on Saturday and Wednesday evenings produced before large audiences the farce "Lord Richard in the Pantry," by Sydney Blow and Douglas Hoare, from the novel of the same name by Martin Swayne.

The rise of the curtain discloses Lord Richard and his manservant, Carter. The former is undergoing "treatment" by having one of his regulation Turkish baths. The conversation shows that he is arranging to "economise" by letting his house and himself taking rooms at the Ritz, and also that whilst serving in Mesopotamia he did some wonderful work which he cannot define and his frequent reference to which always raises a smile on the part of listeners.

Lord Richard is embedded in some big financial undertaking, and quite unintentionally he becomes engaged to the designing Evelyn Lovejoy. The house is let to Sylvia Gayford, a widow, who has a close friend in Lady Violet Elliott. Just as the "change-over" is taking place the financial undertaking in which Lord Richard is interested arouses suspicion so serious that his secretary is despatched to Ireland to make investigations and it becomes necessary that Lord Richard should himself disappear for a time.

Mrs. Gayford lacks a butler, and the cook resents this so much that the cook threatens to leave. Lord Richard develops the idea of becoming the butler in order to disappear, and obtains the position in the name of Bloggins, wearing side whiskers to effect a disguise. Both Mrs. Gayford and Lady Violet know very well that Bloggins is the rightful owner of the house in which he is butler, but cook doesn't and she makes loves to Richard and decides to stay on. Richard is in love with his mistress, and his mistress is in love with him. Much of the fun arises from the circumstance that he often forgets his disguise when in her presence, and that she never does.

Musbury Church Amateur Dramatic Society was formed in 1897 and gave plays regularly in the National School and at other Sunday schools in Haslingden. The picture was taken in October, 1927, when the society gave "Lord Richard in the Pantry." In the opening scene are Harold Taylor, Jim Waite and Albert Taylor.

Peculiar incidents rouse suspicion on the part of the household staff, with the result that when a detective comes to make investigations of whatever Lord Richard may have left behind when, as was thought, he went away, he is denounced by them as the missing culprit. The detective announces that that is simply unbelievable because Lord Richard died the previous night in Ireland, not knowing that it was the secretary who was dead. Of course, everything comes right in the end. Lord Richard is cleared from suspicion, and makes good the losses of members of the household staff who had invested money in the undertaking in which he had been interested. He finds that Mrs. Gayford had all along known who he was and, more important, that she reciprocates his feelings.

The book has one weakness. The decision of Lord Richard to take duty in his own pantry and in the service of a lady he had previously known may possibly be excused as one arrived at in moments of desperation, but it could hardly have happened in actual life without much more careful preparation than he has made.

The characters were taken as follow:—Lord Richard Sandridge, Mr. James W. Waite; Arthur Thompson (his secretary), Mr. A. Taylor; Captain "Tubby" Bannister. Mr. A. McWilton; Carter (Lord Richard's manservant), Mr. H. Taylor; Detective Insp. Brown (Scotland Yard), Mr. I. Jackson; Evelyn Lovejoy, Miss E. Huggett; Lady Violet Elliott, Miss B. Tomlinson; Cook, Miss B. Metcalfe, Rose. Miss B. Ramsbottom, Bryan. Mrs. H. Taylor, Gladys, Miss L. Ashworth (servants of Mrs. Gayford); Sylvia Gayford (a widow), Miss M. Wallwork.

The farce was excellently produced throughout, and was thoroughly enjoyed. In the part of Lord Richard. Mr. James W. Waite, carried the burden of the work. In the opening scene everything depended upon his facial expression, and here and in later scenes he proved a perfect artiste. Miss M. Wallwork, as Mrs. Gayford, was natural. Miss B. Tomlinson seemed rather to overplay the part of Lady Violet, but possibly this was with a view to giving contrast, and there was certainly finish in her work. Miss E. Huggett had a different part as Evelyn Lovejoy, and got through it admirably. The scene between her and Mr. Waite was rich in humour. Mr. H. Taylor, as Carter. Miss M. Metcalfe as cook and Mrs. H. Taylor as Bryan, the parlour-maid, merit special mention, but there was an evenness of excellence in the work of all.

Mr. J. J. Hargreaves conducted an orchestra, which rendered selections during the evening, and Mr. D. Jackson took the duties of stage manager. The Rev. A. Winfield, vicar, is president, Mr. J. W. Waite, secretary, and Mr. J. J. Hargreaves, treasurer of the Society, whose next production we shall look forward to with interest.

MUSBURY SCHOOLS,

—o: HELMSHORE. :o—

ON SATURDAY, FEB. 19TH, 1887,

AN ENTERTAINMENT

CONSISTING OF

 TABLEAUX

SONGS, ETC.,

Will be given in the above Schools, in Aid of the
Church and School Jubilee Fund.

PRICES—

FRONT SEATS, 1s.; SECOND SEATS, 6D.
A FEW RESERVED SEATS, 2s.

DOORS open at 7 o'clock, to Commence at 7-30 p.m.

NEILL, MACHINE PRINTER, DEARDEN-GATE, HASLINGDEN.

—: PROGRAMME. :—

TABLEAUX.

1. The Queen of Hearts.
2. Darby and Joan.
     Song ... ... Mr. H. Greenwood.
3. Trial Scene from the Merchant of Venice.
4. Queen Margaret and the Robber.
     Song... ... ... Mr. Farrell.
5. Joan of Arc at the Stake.
     Reading ... Rev. G. Lomas.
6. A Gipsy Encampment.
7. Amy Robsart and the Earl of Leicester.
     Scene from "The Hunchback." ...
          Miss E. & Mr. C. Lord.
8. Autolycus.
9. Prince Arthur and Hubert. (King John).
     Song... ... ...Mr. Farrell.
10. Scene from Faust.
11. King Alfred in the Neatherd's Hut.
     Song..." I must go a hunting to day"
          Mr. A. Hardman.
12. Robin Hood and his Merry Men.
13. Scene from the Lancashire Witches.

RULES

OF THE

Musbury Friendly Burial Society

HELD AT THE

NATIONAL SCHOOL-ROOM

HELMSHORE

" Bear ye one another's burdens, and so fulfil the law of Christ."

" True Charity is an active principle, and the bond of social life."

FRIENDS AND FELLOW MEMBERS,

We are instructed by our Blessed Redeemer to " love our neighbour as ourselves," and every son and daughter of Adam, is our neighbour, to whom we have it in our power to do good : and as our stations in life are so diversified, by the all-directing hand of a Divine Providence, that we may assist each other in the time of need, it becomes our duty so to do, as far as in us lies.

The plan now recommended is to join together in social compact, and by trifling pecuniary Contributions, enable each other, in times of family bereavement, decently " to bury our dead out of sight." Thus, whilst we engage to help each other we render ourselves individually independent, and can rest satisfied with the consolation, that when death visits our domestic circle, the dying are assured of a decent interment, without becoming a burden to surviving relatives, or dependent on parish relief.

Our plan affords relief unto the poor,
For which they need not beg from door to door.

The Musbury Friendly Burial Society was formed in 1833 and until its merger with the Nottingham Oddfellows Friendly Society in 1992, never increased the contribution of a weekly pre-decimal halfpenny. The message above is from the original prospectus.

Name of Society and place of Registered Office

The Society shall be called " THE MUSBURY FRIENDLY BURIAL SOCIETY." Its registered office shall be the National School, Helmshore, in the county of Lancaster.

Objects of the Society

This Society is established to provide a fund by voluntary subscriptions of the members, together with entrance fees, interest and fines, for the purpose of insuring money to be paid on the death of a member, or for the funeral expenses of a member's child.

Terms of Admission of Members

Any person in good health and approved of by the Committee, from the age of sixteen to thirty years, may be admitted a member of this society on paying three-pence entrance fee and one half-penny per week contributions. Any person from thirty to forty years of age, by approval of the Committee, by paying sixpence entrance fee and one penny per week contributions ; but no person shall be admitted a member who is over forty years of age. Any person entering this society whose

Fines and Forfeitures

Any member neglecting to pay his contributions for three monthly meetings shall pay a fine of one halfpenny and omitting to pay the fourth month a fine of three-halfpence.

Appointment of Committee, Trustees, and other Officers

Any member residing within a radius of three miles from Hollin Bank refusing to serve on the Committee shall be fined two shillings and sixpence, but shall not be liable to serve again for the term of one year. The same person shall not be Secretary or Treasurer and a Trustee of the Society.

Misconduct

Any member or members vilifying or abusing the Secretary, Treasurer, or any other member of the Committee, shall for the first offence be fined sixpence, for the second one shilling, and for the third offence be excluded, and forfeit all moneys paid in.

STAKE LANE.   HELMSHORE.

Primitive Methodism, which aimed at reviving the spirit of John Wesley's early followers, took root in the district about 1820. One of the first meeting places in Helmshore was a room above a shop at Hollin Bank, seen in the photograph on the left next to the Mechanics' Arms (later the Royal British Legion Club). The first Sion Chapel (above right) was opened in 1840 and rebuilt (top left) in 1895. It was demolished in 1982

Leisure activities at Sion Sunday School. The picture top left was taken on January 25, 1930, when the concert included a performance of the sketch "Anastasia joins t' Domino Club."

Top right: "HMS Sion" in 1935. The minister is Mr. Targett. Left: Flag dance at the Christmas "At Home" in 1923. Above: The 1st Helmshore Company, Girls' Life Brigade in 1932. The minister is Mr. Watkins.

Sion and Springhill chapels amalgamated as Helmshore Methodist Church in August 1962. The new church continued the many activities of its predecessors, and in 1964 started a new tradition with the annual crowning of a harvest queen. The photographs show the Christmas concert 1966, and Sandra Haworth, harvest queen in 1968, with her retinue.

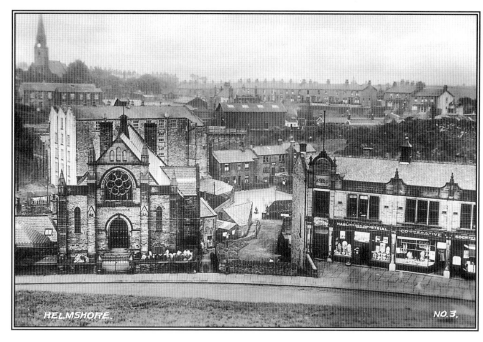

The Helmshore Co-operative Society was formed in 1861 with 27 members and £50 capital. The first shop was in Tanpits. By 1867 the society was prosperous enough to build its own premises fronting Holcombe Road, with a cellar below in Station Road. The photograph (top left) shows the shops in 1904 shortly before the move to new and larger premises next to Sion Chapel. The picture on the left shows the society's officers and a decorated lorry in 1920. The society merged with that in Haslingden in 1931.

New Wesleyan Methodist
SUNDAY SCHOOL,
HELMSHORE.

The Foundation Stone

Of the above School will be placed
On Saturday, June 28th, 1890, at 3 p. m.,

BY

Mrs. G. ASHWORTH SMITH,

OF WESTBOURNE, HELMSHORE,

Who will be supported by

G. A. SMITH, Esq. J. P., THOMAS K. SMITH, Esq.,
JOHN WARBURTON, Esq., J. P., W. H. SMITH, Esq.,
JOSEPH BECKETT, Esq., C. C.,
VERNON STOTT, Esq., and T. B. HAMILTON, Esq.

The Scholars & Friends

Will assemble in the Old School at 2 p. m.,

AND PROCEED IN PROCESSION

To the Site at 2-30 p. m.

The following Ministers will be present and take part
in the proceedings :
Rev. T. BRACKENBURY, (Chairman of the Bolton District,)
Rev. J. V. B. SHREWSBURY, of Rawtenstall,
Rev. W. LEE, Rev. W. C. ANNESLEY, Rev. J. T. DENT,
Rev. J. YEARSLEY, Rev. R. J. ANDREW,
Rev. J. B. NORTON, Rev. J. CHAPPLE,
and Rev. H. W. PATES.

AT 4-30 P.M., TEA WILL BE PROVIDED

in the Old School Room.   Tickets : Adults 1s. each.
Children under 12 years 9d. each.

AFTER TEA,

A PUBLIC MEETING

will be held in the Chapel. Chair to be taken at 7 p. m.,

BY JOSEPH BECKETT, ESQ., C. C.

Addresses will be given by the above Ministers & other Friends.

A Collection will be taken at the Stone Laying and at the
close of the Public Meeting, in aid of the Building Funds.
Your presence and support are respectfully solicited.

James Theodore Donaldson, Printer, Haslingden.

WESLEYAN CHAPEL & SCHOOL,   HELMSHORE.

Wesleyan Methodism was a powerful force in Helmshore, particularly in the second half of the 19th century and the first half of the 20th. The first meeting place was Fold House, Gregory Fold, which was used until 1855. A Sunday school was built at Springhill in 1841 and was replaced by the building in the picture in 1891. The chapel was opened in 1867 and both buildings were used until amalgamation with Sion church in August 1962.

The Sunday school was a centre of social as well as religious life, as can be seen from the following pages.

H.W.S.S. XMAS 1921. Photo Constantine.

Concerts at Springhill Wesleyan Sunday School in the 1920s. The concert party (top left) was formed by John Edward Wolstenholme, second from the right. The picture above was taken in about 1924.

WESLEYAN SCHOOL, ERECTED 1891

IF YOU ATTEND NO OTHER PLACE OF WORSHIP —

YOU ARE *Heartily Welcome* TO ATTEND THE

WESLEYAN CHAPEL or SUNDAY SCHOOL

Changing fashions. About 50 years separate the two photographs taken outside Springhill Sunday School. The older group posed at the turn of the century, the other in 1947. On the right is the Rev. F. Gordon Mee, a popular minister in the early 1930s.

Helmshore Amateur Operatic Society

WILL PRESENT

GILBERT & SULLIVAN'S OPERA

"RUDDIGORE"

(By permission of R. D'Oyly Carte, Esq.)

IN THE

Musbury Church School, Helmshore,

On Saturdays Jan. 17th & 24th, at 7 o/c
and Wednesday, Jan. 21st, at 7.30 p.m.

Seats 2/- (Reserved), 1/6 and 1/-

Plan of Seats open January 10th, at
T. B. Hargreaves, Stationer, Helmshore.

☞ IN AID OF LOCAL CHARITIES.

After the First World War, members of Helmshore Wesleyan Choir staged a number of operettas and by 1926 felt confident enough to present "The Gondoliers" by Gilbert and Sullivan. A scene from the production is reproduced above. In the following year, the Helmshore Liberal Operatic Society was formed (most Wesleyans were Liberals) and another G. & S. favourite, "The Pirates of Penzance" was given at Springhill (left). Soon the whole village became enthusiastic for light opera and the Helmshore Amateur Operatic Society came into being. The production of "Ruddigore" was given in 1931.

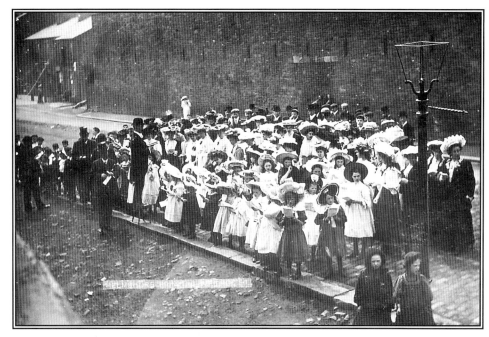

Tanpits. The photograph (top left) was taken in 1906. The houses on the right - Spring Gardens, otherwise Hencote Row - were built in the 1820s, at the same time as Middle Mill opposite. The mill was originally seven storeys high. Top right: Primitive Methodist procession in 1910 and left, the Musbury Church procession in 1908. All three pictures show "Little Bobby's Shop" (now demolished). Little Bobby was Robert Birtwistle (right) who carried on the grocery business for many years.

Helmshore from Tanner Bank: a photograph taken during the demolition of the octagonal Middle Mill chimney in August, 1956. The old man on the right is John Mitchell, whose sister Betty Ashworth ran Middle Mill during the third quarter of the last century and who left him the row of houses adjoining the Conservative Club. He ran a shop (now demolished, see picture on page 74) and measured lengths of twist tobacco by wrapping them once round his neck. Late in life he developed an interest in astronomy and is reputed to have climbed Tanner Bank with the intention of touching the moon with a clothes prop. In 1900, when over 80, he lit the bonfire built on Tor to celebrate the Relief of Mafeking.

USING HIS LOAF

Of all the time-saving products of recent years, sliced bread stands high. Somebody, almost certainly an American, has made a fortune out of it. The inventor, his backers and bakeries around the world probably looked on the first bread slicer as a wonderfully new idea. If that is what they thought they were wrong. Let me put the record straight by recording for posterity some account of one Alexander Lindsay, power-loom overlooker and inventor, who turned his fertile mind to the automatic slicing of bread in the years immediately before the First World War.

Like many "tacklers", who spent their working lives maintaining the cotton looms of Lancashire, Alexander Lindsay devoted his leisure hours to making things. His workshop was the cellar of his home, a terraced house in Spring Bank, Helmshore. There, helped occasionally by his neighbour, Hebert Simm, office boy at a local mill, he tried to turn his dreams into hard cash. Among his many inventions was a multiple bread slicer, a device so intimidating that old villagers still speak of it with awe.

The idea for a bread slicer occurred to Alexander at a Sunday school tea party, one of those popular village events at which immense quantities of bread and butter were consumed. The ladies of the Sion Primitive Methodist Chapel, of which Alexander was a prominent member, were delighted to hear that he had begun work on a device which would take the strain from their aching arms and fingers.

Mrs. Lindsay was less enthusiastic. She it was who had to bake the loaves upon which her husband experimented.

Alexander was ambitious. Not for him a machine that cut a slice at a time. The instant transformation of a large loaf into neat and equal slices became his single aim. Large knives were arranged in line and brought down in unison to guillotine the bread. That the machine failed to live up to the expectations of its inventor none who saw it in action will deny. The slices were anything but straight and never once achieved that neat and slender look so essential for a Sunday school tea party. Often whole loaves would be terribly mangled, leaving debris that could not be eaten even in the family circle. Mrs. Lindsay rebelled and the bread slicer was put aside – an idea years before its time – and the inventive Alexander turned his attention to making gas mantles.

When these also proved a failure, he returned once more to slicing bread, using a single blade. This much more modest machine was an unqualified success. To the ladies of the chapel, however, it seemed a fearsome thing and they refused to risk their fingers by operating it.

Alexander thereupon appointed himself chapel bread slicer and over the years reached speeds that were astonishing. Loaves were instantly converted into beautiful slices, which the ladies were happy to butter. On Alexander's death, Joe, his son, carried on the tradition, carefully dismantling the machine and cleaning each component after every tea party. When he died, no one felt skilled enough to step into his shoes. But by that time, sliced loaves were beginning to appear in the shops.

Chris Aspin
Reproduced from "Lancashire Life"

Middle Mill tacklers in the 1890s. On the right is Alexander Lindsay, pioneer of sliced bread, whose story is told in the accompanying article.

❖ TOASTS. ❖

1.—Her Most Gracious Majesty the Queen.

National Anthem—Solo, Mr. F. A. Robinson.

2.—H.R.H. the Prince and Princess of Wales
and the rest of the Royal Family.

Song ... ... Mr. W. Sharples.

Song ... ... Mr. Geo. Burke.

3.—Success to the Helmshore Manufacturing
Company, Limited.

Song ... ... Mr. James Howarth.

Song ... ... Mr. F. A. Robinson.

4.—The Visiting Friends.

Song ... ... Mr. Paulson.

Song ... ... Mr. R. H. Kay.

Song ... ... Mr. Wm. Greenwood.

5.—The Directors and Shareholders of the
Helmshore Manufacturing Co., Ltd.

Song ... ... Mr. W. Sharples.

Duett ... Messrs. Robinson & Greenwood.

Song ... ... Mr. Geo. Burke.

6.—The Overlookers of the Helmshore Manufacturing Company, Limited.

Song ... ... Mr. F. A. Robinson.

Song ... Mr. Tom Wolstenholme.

Song ... ... Mr. Jno. Greenwood.

7.—The Host and Hostess.

Glee ... Middle Mill Glee Party.

Song ... ... Mr. George Burke.

Song ... ... Mr. F. A. Robinson.

GOD SAVE THE QUEEN.

— THE —

HELMSHORE MANUFACTURING CO., LD.,

HELMSHORE.

SHAREHOLDERS' ANNUAL

DINNER,

JANUARY 19, 1901.

MANAGING DIRECTOR: MR. R. H. KAY.

SECRETARY: MR. KENDAL CHEW.

Middle Mill, Helmshore.

Victoria Mill, Ramsbottom.

❖ MENU. ❖

SOUPS.

HARE AND OXTAIL.

FISH.

TURBOT AND LOBSTER SAUCE.

JOINTS.

ROAST RIB OF BEEF.

ROAST MUTTON—ONION SAUCE.

FOWLS.

ROAST TURKEY—SAUSAGES.

ROAST DUCK—APPLE SAUCE.

ROAST AND BOILED CHICKEN.

VEAL AND RABBIT PIE.

GAME.

PHEASANTS.

SWEETS.

PLUM AND CABINET PUDDINGS.

DAMSON, APPLE, AND MINCE TARTS.

CUSTARDS, JELLIES, &c.

CHEESE AND CELERY.

DESSERT.

PINES, GRAPES, APPLES, ORANGES, BANANAS,
PEARS, WALNUTS, RAISINS, &c.

Geo. Paley, Purveyor.

Lighter moments at Middle Mill. The manager, Mr. Emanuel Shaw, shows that he can still kiss the shuttle. Note the Lancashire looms and the gas mantles in this and the other photograph of the weaving shed. Both were taken in 1906. The picture on the right is of winders in the 1920s.

Tanpits in the 1920s. At the far end of the row are stables used by Mr. Joe Schofield ("Joe Posy") who is pictured above. He sold greengroceries from a horse-drawn cart.
Left: Children from Holden Wood with their home-made maypole in 1923. The photograph was taken near Co-operative Street.

James Barlow and Sons was one of the oldest firms in Helmshore. It began at Sunnybank fulling woollen cloth, but moved to the entrance to the Musbury valley after Joseph Porritt bought the original mill. The Barlows renamed the former dyeworks at Tanpits "Sunnybank Mill", so that for more than a century there were two mills in the village with the same name. Barlow's switched from wool to cotton on moving from Alden. The firm was bought out by a Westhoughton company in 1979 and the mill closed a few years later. It was demolished piecemeal between 1985 and 1987.

The mill was powered by Helmshore's last steam engine which can be seen above. Named "Joseph Arthur", it ran for nearly 100 years. The photograph on the left shows Managing Director, Mr. Frank Ashworth, stopping the engine for the last time on July 22, 1960.

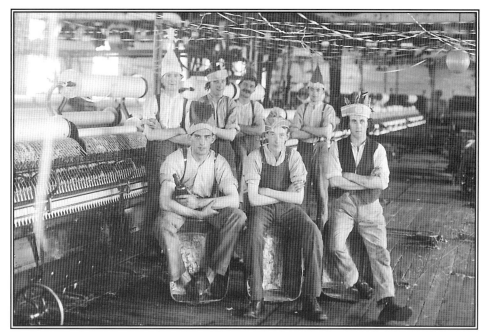

Workers at Barlow's Sunnybank Mill. The photographs show weavers and mule spinners celebrating Christmas in 1921 and a presentation in 1937 to the retiring general manager, Mr. Fred Barlow.

Lodge Bank. The upper left picture shows the old building which was once a smithy and which was later used as a gynasium by the Hollin brothers (see following page). It was replaced by the row of houses shown in the lower photograph in 1911. The small building on the opposite side of the road was a fish and chip shop. Above right: 1911 Coronation celebrations on the Holme Field. Below right: Weavers from Middle Mill enjoying a fish and chip dinner in about 1924.

Weightlifting enjoyed a spell of great popularity in Helmshore at the turn of the century, thanks largely to Charles Hollin, who was the Lancashire champion in 1899. Mr. Hollin and his brother William, both mill workers, ran the Hollin School of Physical Culture in an old building (see page 82), the site of which is now occupied by Lodge Bank. Village lads were put to work on dumbells and chest expanders before moving on to kettle weights and bar-bells. The above photograph is a studio portrait of the Hollin Trio - Christopher Wise, Charles Hollin and William Hollin - at the height of their fame as public entertainers. On the right is Charles Hollin supporting a dumbell of nearly 250 lb.

Officers of Musbury Church at the bottom of Gregory Fold during a Whitsuntide procession in the early '20s. It was customary for Mr. William Whittaker (extreme right) to distribute oranges to all the walkers at this point. Mr. Whittaker was a partner in the firm of L. & W. Whittaker, fulling millers, of Higher Mill. The door on the right of the picture led onto his land.

Village blacksmiths. The smithy was on the riverside opposite Park Mill. The above photograph, taken in the early 1890s, shows Andrew McQuilton and his apprentices. Above left (in shirtsleeves) is Mr. Sam Egerton, who spent his working life at the smithy, which he bought in 1908 and ran until his retirement in 1953. Shoeing horses was an important part of the business. The picture was taken in 1940. Posters on the smithy advertise the Palace and Empire Cinemas at Haslingden, a cricket match at Bentgate, a sale of cotton machinery at Bacup, church services, Andrew's Liver Salt and a funfair.

Mr. Sam Egerton in his smithy in Holcombe Road. The "striker" is his apprentice, Joe Seddon, of Westhoughton. The photograph was taken in August 1948.

Above left: Mr. Lawrence Whittaker, of the firm of L. and W. Whittaker, fulling millers, Higher Mill: a photograph taken in 1900. Mr. Whittaker was known as Helmshore's best-dressed man and he also cultivated one of the best greenhouses in the district. In 1894, Mr. Whittaker won Helmshore Ward for the Conservatives by one vote. He and his Liberal opponent, Mr. J. H. Spencer, had previously agreed to vote for each other, but on polling day Mr. Whittaker changed his mind and voted for himself.

Above: Mr. Benjamin Haworth, better known as Ben o' Rabbits, who, like Mr. Whittaker, was a mill owner, Conservative councillor and warden of Musbury Church. He came to Helmshore in 1880 to manage Park Mill, the 1893 extension of which can be seen in the photograph on the left. He later became sole owner of the mill. Mr. Haworth and Mr. W. J. Porritt were the first Helmshore representatives (in 1883) on the extended Haslingden Local Board. He was a founder of Helmshore Conservative Club and a keen supporter of the village band.

The photograph on the left was taken in about 1910 at a point near Mr. Whittaker's greenhouse.

Bottling home-grown fruit at Industrial Terrace. Arthur Constantine's photograph of Mrs. Sarah Constantine (seated) and her housekeeper, Miss Mitchell, was taken in 1933. A CWS calendar and a Methodist tract hang on the walls. Note the wireless on the piano. The programmes on the right were broadcast in March 1933.

NATIONAL PROGRAMME (1,554 m.).

10-15—Service.
10-30—Weather.
10-40—11-0—"The World in a Mirror."
12-0—Haydn Heard's Band, from West End Cinema Birmingham.
1-0—Reginald New: Organ of Beaufort Cinema, Washwood Heath, Birmingham.
1-45—Grosvenor House Orchestra, from Grosvenor House, Park Lane.
2-25—For Schools.
3-45—Music of French Composers. Scottish Studio Orchestra.
4-30—Reginald Dixon: Organ of Tower Ballroom, Blackpool.
5-15—Children's Hour.
6-0—News.
6-25—Interlude.
6-30—Foundations of Music, played by Leslie England.
6-55—"New Books": Mr. R. Ellis Roberts.
7-15—"Man v. Microbe." Measles.
7-30—"Some Makers of the Modern Spirit."—X. Mr. Geoffrey Sainsbury: "Nietzche."
8-0—B.B.C. Chamber Concerts.—VII. Kutcher String Quartet. William Murdoch (Pianoforte).
9-0—News.
9-20—"Other People's Houses."—XI. Sir Raymond Unwin.
9-35—"Seven Days' Sunshine." Musical Cruise: Book and Lyrics by Henrik Ege. Music by Norman Hackforth.
10-35—"Deirdre," by James Stephens, read by Cecil Ramage.
10-40—12-0—Harry Roy's Band, relayed from relayed from Cafe Anglais.

NORTH REGIONAL (480 m.).

10-15—Service.
10-30—Daventry National Programme.
10-45—11-0—"The Week-end": Mr. N. E. Moore Raymond—"Up Swaledale."
12-0—Sydney Gustard: Organ of Gaumont Palace Cinema, Chester.
1-0—Daventry National Programme.
3-5—Recital of Gramophone Records.
3-30—Midland Studio Orchestra. George Gibbs (Baritone).
4-45—Daventry National Programme.
5-15—Children's Hour.
6-0—News.
6-30—Yorkshire Mummers.
7-15—Mr. F. Stacey Lintott: The Month in Northern Sport.
7-30—Wiliam Rees Concert, from Free Trade Hall, Manchester. Arthur Catterall (Violin); Manchester Philharmonic Choir and Orchestra.
9-0—Interval, including Gramophone Records from the Studio.
9-15—Concert (continued).
10-15—News.
10-30—12-0—Dance Music: Ambrose's Orchestra, from May Fair Hotel.

Holcombe Road. The photographs of the Wesleyan procession at Higher Mill and the Musbury procession near Co-operative Street were taken in about 1908. The lower pictures are of Weir Foot ("Wedge Row") in 1907 and the cottages at Holden Wood, which were demolished in 1976.

Early vehicles in Holcombe Road. Above left: Mr. Ross Whittaker in his 1921 Austin shortly after its purchase. Left: Haslingden Fire Brigade with their Leyland fire engine at Higher Mill. The vehicle was registered at Bury in January, 1921. The house above was the home of Mr. and Mrs. William Whittaker before they moved to Woodlands at Top o' th' Brow. Mrs. Whittaker was famous in the village for the spick and span appearance of her property. The steps, wall and windowsills were masterpieces of donkey-stone art and she is said to have taken the rockery indoors at least once a year to be washed. Note the aspidistras.

Cams Mill, now demolished, in about 1910. It was used by the woollen firm of Stott and Smith for fulling, raising, dyeing and finishing. The business was founded in Edenfield by James Stott and Thomas Smith and transferred to Haslingden when Stott built Sykeside Mill in 1836. Smith came to Helmshore at the age of 13 to learn the woollen business with George Ashworth, of Gregory Fold. In his later years he lived at Turfcote. His second son, George Ashworth Smith, rebuilt Flaxmoss House.

HIGHER MILL VIADUCT, HELMSHORE IN 1848

SPORT and LEISURE

Dan Gregory, cyclist and athlete, a photograph of 1896. He once ran down Helmshore Road, through the station booking office and cleared the railway lines with a prodigious leap.

Grand
FOOTBALL MATCH.

Helmshore v. Irwell Springs.

Semi-Final Shield Tie.

On Saturday, February the Sixteenth,
A Football match was played;
Both teams they met for Rossendale Shield
On Stake Lane ground that day.

And Irwell Springs, they brought a tape,
By which to measure goals;
Four inches cut out, together stuck.
By a player I was told.

And referee to them request
If a protest they had laid,
They said too narrow were the goals,
Before they started play.

So they measured them by Irwell's tape,
But the numbers they were wrong,
Haslam and Barnes brought measurement
Which made them twirl their tongue.

But referee said they were right:
When lookers-on heard that,
Some of Springs lot were in such a way,
They jumped like Bacup cats.

Now both teams seem in equal strength,
In build, in size, and weight;
To compete for this Rossendale shield,
They only thought it reight.

The home team they win the toss,
Wind in their favour play.
The Springs in coloured jerseys are,
The home team as light as day.

So now the sphere in centre put,
The players in their place,
The ball kick off, away they go
Towards the Springs' goal chase.

The Irwell defenders kicked it back,
But Holden's on the watch,
Who kicks the ball to centre play,
As now the forwards scratch.

And down the field they make a rush,
They come in eager force,
The ball is passed from man to man,
To the wing takes its course.

As now the home team they do press
And Dean, who has the ball,
Pass it to Hargreaves, outside wing,
Who shot it through the goal.

This now receives tremendous cheers.
The Spectators in full glee,
With many a shout, 'now play up, lads,'
'You'll win, I do believe.'

Excitement grew to such a pitch,
And both John Willies on the field,
I believe they fairly did give meauth
When they yerd it were for Rossendale Shield.

And now they change, to Springs' delight,
Who think they have the game,
The ball kicked off, and down the field,
A corner kick they claim.

That lad Bill Honey there you see,
And Heys is in the goal;
Harry Eastwood got the ball away,
Their opponents charge and fall

And Springs they showed their level best
To dodge and pass down field;
Fedden and Crabtree they were there,
Played up for Rossendale Shield.

And now young Ross sent in some shots
He played just like a tar,
Both Bennies run it up the wing,
Sent it across the bar.

The Visitors' goal was now attacked,
He just managed to save;
The Springs' forwards rush down and score,
So neither side does wave.

The home team like the light brigade
Towards the goal they dash,
Besieged, attack, they onward rushed,
Both man and ball went splash.

The whistle blows, the play at end,
I'm sure with me confess,
Of all the matches that's been played,
This is one of the best.

SPECTATOR.

When Mr. James Stott laid the foundation stone of Springhill Wesleyan Chapel in 1866, he looked back to the days when the chief winter sport of Helmshore people was "running down hares and tracking their footprints in the snow." Times had changed, however, and he was glad to say that the three village Sunday schools had brought about a great improvement in the condition of the inhabitants.

The sportsmen of Helmshore were no longer the "Musbury Turks" remembered by Mr. Stott. Young men were turning to more traditional games. A cricket club was formed in 1869 and a football club in the 1880s. The adjacent broadsheet describes the footballers' triumph in the semi-final of the Rossendale Charity Shield competition of 1889. The Stake Lane ground was near the White Horse. The club won the final by defeating Rossendale Reserves 4 - 2 on the Haslingden F.C. ground behind the Clarence Hotel, Flaxmoss.

The affinity of football and the arts in Helmshore was evident again in November 1889, when a well-attended concert was given in Musbury National School to raise money for the club. No occasion this for a boisterous sing-song: the proceedings opened said the *Rossendale Free Press*, with the village headmaster, Mr. W. B. Yates, giving a well-executed performance of a piano sonata by Dussek.

The village cricket club had only a short life, but in the present century, the three churches entered teams in the Haslingden Sunday School League.

Football has always been a popular sport in Helmshore and several clubs have fielded teams. Above is the Helmshore United side of 1904. It played at Cockham. Above right: Helmshore Albion, in 1912. The ground was between Ravenshore and Irwell Vale. Holding the ball is J. T. Fowles. Right, a later Helmshore United formed after the First World War and known as "The Terribles." This side played at Iron Gate.

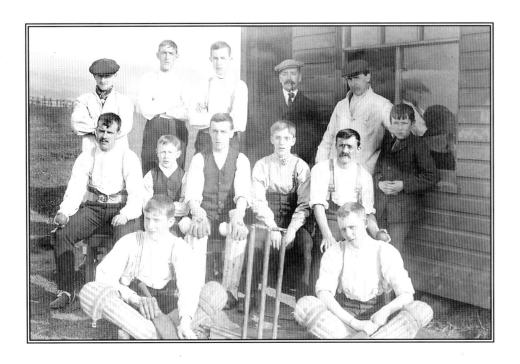

Springhill Wesleyan cricketers in the first decade of the century. The field was on Fairhill, now crossed by Cherry Tree Way. The club played in the Haslingden Sunday School League and had its own pavilion. Later a square was laid. Crown green bowling has long been a popular sport in Helmshore, with the Liberal Club the main centre. The bowlers are Mr. Jack Nutter (left) and Mr. Ephraim Nutter.

Races to the top of Tor and back were run from the Holme Field (now partly covered by the offices of Airtours) on red letter days before the First World War. In 1958, the Helmshore Local History Society revived the race, which became known as the Tor Mile and which was started from Barlow Terrace. At first the race was limited to local runners, but as its fame spread, members of athletic clubs were increasingly attracted by the challenge. The picture (left) shows the Mayor of Haslingden, Councillor W. B. Fisher, presenting the cup for the senior race to John Robinson on June 21, 1958. His time was 9 minutes 10 seconds. Top left: Stanley Bradshaw winning the race in 1960. Top centre: Bill Grimshaw first to the top of the hill in that year. Above: Runners in the 1958 race approaching the steepest part of the climb. The best time for the race during the seven years it was run by the society was 8 minutes, 1.4 secs. by the England international runner Brian Hall, of Manchester, in 1963.

Helmshore Band was formed in 1872 and quickly became a village institution. Its first success was at the Crawshawbooth Contest of 1906 and the photograph above left shows the bandsmen and their supporters at Sunnybank after their triumphant return in a wagonette. In 1909 the band bought 24 uniforms with red collars and red cuffs. A suit and cap cost 22s 6d. The picture on the left was taken on the Liberal Club bowling green shortly after the new uniforms arrived. Above: The band heading the procession to mark the Coronation of King George V in 1911.

HELMSHORE PRIZE BAND 1921. A CONSTANTINE.

HELMSHORE BAND'S SUCCESSES.

There was great rejoicing at Helmshore on Saturday upon Helmshore Prize Band following its success of a few weeks ago by at Stalybridge taking the first prize—£15 15s. and challenge cup, value ten guineas, as well as two members of the band, Robt. Wadylove and Frank Tattersall, carrying off the medals for euphonium and trombone solos respectively. This is the second occasion within a few weeks upon which Mr. Tattersall, who is a local man, has carried off a medal in test-piece playing. The success of the band reflects great credit upon Mr. Richard Aspin, who has trained the band and was conductor in the contest. The judge (Mr. J. Brier, Yorkshire) said the tone, time, and precision of the band were excellent. He complimented Mr. Aspin on his reading of the piece, and extracting from it all the possible points. The other prize-winners at the contest were: Second, and horn medal, Thornsett (conductor, F. Barber); 3rd, and cornet medal, Eccles Borough (Wm. Halliwell); 4th, and trombone medal (W. Scholes); 5th, Hollingworth (W. Rhodes). The unsuccessful bands were: Compstall, Oldham Postal, Oldham Rifles, Dobcross, and Park Vale Public; ten bands competing.

Helmshore Band photographed in 1921 at Tor Side House, home of the President, Mr. Oliver Porritt, who is seated next to bandmaster, Mr. Richard Aspin. The band won the Stalybridge contest in both 1920 and 1921. Above right: The band and supporters leaving Helmshore for the Irlam Contest of August 21, 1920, when it won second prize.

A Few Wrong Notes

Some odd entries from old minute-books of the Helmshore Prize Brass Band are reprinted in the autumn edition of "The Helmshore Historian." "Any alteration of any kind to the bandmaster," says one stern note. "shall be left to Mr Tattersall." and there is another asking for a player "to go on solo cornet, if he can see his way." The decision "to have elastic bands for music" is understandable enough, but what astonishing enterprise lies behind the minute which says simply: "Moved that Mr Tomkins and Mr Tomlinson be in charge of the Israelites crossing the Red Sea"?

In spite of their modest speeds, the early motor buses and char-a-bancs were regarded as an adventurous means of locomotion and a trip in one was often the occasion for a photograph. The Station Hotel outing in 1908 was among the first from the village. Above left: A Porritts trip to Southport in 1920 and left, the Springhill Mothers ready to set off from the chapel in the same year.

TEMPERANCE and DRINK

B.W. TEMPERANCE ASSOCIATION

Drinkers and non-drinkers. A party from the Bridge End Hotel visiting the Three Fishes, Mitton, at the beginning of the century. The accordionist is Mr. Alf Bedford, signalman at Helmshore for many years. The ladies, all members of the British Women's Temperance Association, were photographed at Sion Chapel in about 1907. The Band of Hope card of 1898 warns that strong drink is "a biting, stinging serpent, something evil, to be feared, hated, and fought against as long as we live."

Church of England
Temperance Society.
MUSBURY BRANCH.

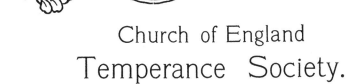

Annual Tea Party and Concert

WILL BE HELD ON

SATURDAY, DEC 4th, 1915,

Tea on the Tables at 4-30 p.m.   Concert to commence at 6-30 p.m.

Chairman: Mr. F. W. Malpass.

Songs, Recitations and Sketches by the Members.

Prices of Admission: Tea and Concert, Adults 9d.,
Children under 14, 6d.   Concert 6d. & 3d.

J. A. BANKS, Secretary
H. STEFF, Treasurer.

Rostron Lord, Printer, Helmshore.

PROGRAMME.

Opening Hymn.

Soldiers of Christ ! arise,
And put your armour on,
Strong in the strength which God
supplies
Through His eternal Son :

Strong in the Lord of Hosts,
And in His mighty power :
Who in the strength of Jesus trusts,
Is more than conqueror !

Stand then, in His great might,
With all His strength endued ;
And take, to arm you for the fight
The panoply of God.

From strength to strength go on,
Wrestle, and fight, and pray,
Tread all the powers of darkness down,
And win the well-fought day

That, having all things done,
And all your conflicts past,
Ye may o'ercome through Christ alone,
And victor stand at last. Amen.

Chairman's Remarks.   Secretary's Report.

Song...	Mr. J. Waite
Song	Master W. Taylor
Action Song "Mr. Gollywog, Good Night" ...	Children
Recitation	Miss N. Entwistle

Temperance Sketch   "The Outcast"   Four Characters

Action Song 'When the boys come marching home'	Girls
Recitation	Miss M. Wallwork
Song	Master A. Taylor

Humorous Sketch   "Father's Mistake"   Five Characters

Action Song "We're all under the same old Flag"	Girls
Song	Master A. Taylor
Song...	Miss D. Whittam
Action Song "They sang God Save our King"	Boys & Girls

Patriotic Sketch   "England wants them"   Three Characters

The above Sketches are by kind permission of Messrs.
Abel Heywood & Son, Ltd.

The battle against the evils of strong drink was waged unceasingly in Victorian and Edwardian Britain. The temperance advocates fought on many fronts and with many weapons. In Helmshore, there were temperance groups in the three churches and a completely independent body, the Blue Ribbon Club. This was formed in 1882 following a campaign by the Blue Ribbon Army led by an American named Murphy. The club survived until 1932, by which time it was the last of its kind in the country. Drinking members of the community referred to the building in Station Brow as the "Cowd Wather" (Cold Water) club, but once a year, in the week before the annual holiday, its hot water was much in demand, for the cellar held the first and only public bath in Helmshore. The club played an important role in the social life of the village, providing games, newspapers and the occasional concert for a modest subscription. The photograph shows the members in 1919. The president, Mr. Frank Tattersall, is the fifth from the left in the second row.

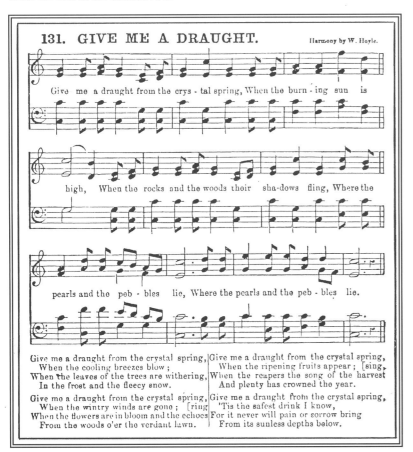

131. GIVE ME A DRAUGHT.   Harmony by W. Hoyle.

Give me a draught from the crys-tal spring, When the burn-ing sun is high, When the rocks and the woods their sha-dows fling, Where the pearls and the peb-bles lie, Where the pearls and the peb-bles lie.

Give me a draught from the crystal spring,	Give me a draught from the crystal spring,
When the cooling breezes blow;	When the ripening fruits appear; [sing,
When the leaves of the trees are withering,	When the reapers the song of the harvest
In the frost and the fleecy snow.	And plenty has crowned the year.
Give me a draught from the crystal spring,	Give me a draught from the crystal spring,
When the wintry winds are gone; [ring	'Tis the safest drink I know,
When the flowers are in bloom and the echoes	For it never will pain or sorrow bring
From the woods o'er the verdant lawn.	From its sunless depths below.

HELMSHORE
BLUE RIBBON CLUB.

COMMITTEE'S CARD.

Oct. 1920—Sept. 1921

President : - F. Tattersall, Esq.

Treasurer : - Wm. Cropper, Esq.

Secretaries :
G. A. Pilkington and F. Barnes

Name

RULES.

1. Every Member is a Pledged Teetotaler. If known otherwise he will be immediately expelled.

2. Subscriptions are payable in advance, every Friday night from 7-30 to 8-0 No Member is allowed to be more than 4 weeks in arrears.

3. Any member leaving the Club must notify the Secretaries before doing so, otherwise he is liable for payments until such notice is given.

4. The Secretaries will not be responsible for payments made unless entered on this card.

5. Any suggestions or complaints are to be given to the Secretaries and will be discussed at the next Committee Meeting.

BLUE RIBBON CLUB,

HELMSHORE.

A

GRAND CONCERT

In aid of the above Club, will be given

IN THE NATIONAL SCHOOL,

On SATURDAY, OCTOBER 7, 1893,

When the following Artistes will appear:—

SOPRANO:

MISS ANNIE HOWARTH, H.V.C., T.C.L.,
Accrington.

TENOR:

MR. DAVID HANSON, T.C.L.,
Haslingden.

BASS:

MR. SHORROCKS,
Accrington.

SOLO VIOLIN:

MISS GORDON NUNN,
Of the Free Trade Hall & Provincial Concerts.

HUMORIST: MR. WILSON

BLACKLEDGE
St. Helens.

SOLO PIANO AND ACCOMPANIST:

MISS E. TAYLOR, A.L.C.M.,
Edenfield.

ADMISSION :- Front Seats, 1s. 6d. ; Second Seats, 1s. ; Back Seats, 6d.
Doors open at 6.30, to commence at 7 p.m. prompt. Tickets may be had from any of the Committee, or at the Door.

PROGRAMME.

PIANOFORTE SOLO		
Miss TAYLOR.		
SONG ... ..."The Pilgrim of Love"... ...		*Bishop*
MR. D. HANSON.		
SONG ... ... "Killarney"		*Balfe*
Miss HOWARTH.		
HUMOROUS SKETCH ... "Our Smoking Concert" ...		
MR. WILSON BLACKLEDGE.		
SONG ... ... "The Village Blacksmith"		*Weiss*
MR. SHORROCKS.		
VIOLIN SOLO ... "Scotch Fantaisie"		*P. Sainton*
Miss GORDON NUNN.		
SONG ... ... "Dream of Home"		*Arditi*
Miss HOWARTH.		
MEDLEY ... ... "Once upon a time"		
MR. WILSON BLACKLEDGE.		
SONG ... ... "The Mighty Deep" ...		*W. H. Jude*
MR. SHORROCKS.		
VIOLIN SOLO ... ... "Faust"		*Sarasate*
Miss GORDON NUNN.		
HUMOROUS SKETCH..."The Village Choir Concert"		
MR. WILSON BLACKLEDGE.		
SONG ... "Come into the Garden, Maud ?" ...		*Balfe*
MR. D. HANSON.		
SONG ... ... "Off to Philadelphia"		
MR. SHORROCKS.		
HUMOROUS SKETCH..."Tommy's Birthday Party" ...		
MR. WILSON BLACKLEDGE.		

J. A. Donaldson, John Street Printing Works, Haslingden.

LANCASHIRE POLICE DISTRICT.

PORTRAIT AND DESCRIPTION OF HABITUAL DRUNKARDS.

Name and alias **THOMAS** *WHITTAKER.*

Residence No 46, Pleasant Street, Haslingden.

Place where employed None.

Age 46 years.

Height 5 ft. 5½ ins.

Build Medium.

Complexion Fresh.

Hair Light Brown, turning grey.

Eyes Grey.

Whiskers } Clean shaven.
Moustache }

Shape of nose Roman, very large and Red.

Shape of face Long.

Peculiarities or marks T. W. compass and square and star left forearm.

Profession or occupation Retired County Court Clerk.

Date and nature of conviction 12th Oct., 1903. Drunk and disorderly at Haslingden. Fined 5/- and Costs.

Court at which convicted Haslingden Petty Session.

N.B.—Should any known Habitual Drunkard attempt to purchase or obtain any intoxicating liquor at any premises licensed for the sale of intoxicating liquor by retail or at the premises of any registered Club it is requested that the licensed person or the person refusing to supply the liquor will, as soon as practicable, give information of such attempt to the Police of the District, in order that the law may be enforced.

To the Licensee of the Robin Hood Inn Haslingdon

To the Secretary of the Registered Club }

The Robin Hood in Holcombe Road and a warning to the landlord about a notorious drunkard of 1903. The photograph was taken in the early years of the century when the landlord was Mr. David Hanson, who is at the door with his wife. As can be seen on the previous page, Mr. Hanson was one of the soloists at the Blue Ribbon Club concert in 1893.

SPECIAL OCCASIONS

June 12, 1909.

LIBERAL GARDEN PARTY AT HELMSHORE

THE SUFFRAGETTES AND MR. L. HARCOURT, M.P.

By the invitation of Mr. and Mrs. O. W. Porritt there was a great gathering of Liberals of Rossendale in the beautiful and spacious grounds of Torr Side, Helmshore, in the Haslingden borough, on Saturday afternoon. Invitations had been issued to over 1,200 ladies and gentlemen in all parts of the Division for a garden party to meet Mr. L. Harcourt, member for the Division and First Commissioner of Works in the Government, and with a beautiful day the invitations were generally responded to.

The announcement of the fete brought representatives of the Women's Social and Political Union into the Division a fortnight ago, for the suffragettes make war on Mr. Harcourt at every opportunity because of his attitude on their question as a Cabinet Minister. They sought to gain admittance to Saturday's party, but admission was strictly by ticket. The idea of gaining admittance as waitresses for the caterers occurred to the women (one of the women told a " Gazette " man); but there also they were foiled, for the organization was so complete that the idea had occurred to Mr. Monks, the Liberal agent, also.

A group of about a dozen of the suffragettes awaited the arrival of Mr. Harcourt by train from Manchester—two of them were on duty five hours before he was due—and there was a big crowd in anticipation of events. Miss Garnett, of Leeds, and Mrs. Morris, of Manchester, met Mr. Harcourt as he alighted and implored him to remove his opposition to the giving of the suffrage to women ere that opposition had cost him his seat. Mr. Harcourt only smiled serenely. Mrs. Baines, however, added hers to the pleas of her comrades, and after that the women threw some of their literature into the carriage. At the station and inside and outside the grounds at Torr Side about two dozen policemen were on duty to, if need be, supplement the work of the numerous stewards, but

in the entire absence of anything that came within their scope the men in blue shared in the good time everybody enjoyed.

Outwitted and foiled, the suffragettes were more turbulent when the party was over and Mr. and Mrs. Harcourt were departing. One of them dashed in front of the carriage driving the hon member and his wife to the station and might have been knocked down and run over had she not been dragged back at a critical moment by one of the stewards. The suffragette concerned denounced Mr. Harcourt as a coward because he would run over a woman who challenged his position. The police were about to clear the railway platform when Mr. Harcourt interposed on behalf of the suffragettes, and afterwards he had a short chat with some of them. Some of the suffragettes got on the same train as Mr. Harcourt and vowed they would get at him at Manchester when he was unprotected.

On the lawn a varied programme was gone through. The Helmshore Prize Band gave selections, with Mr. Jerry Lord as soloist, and there were also " turns " in thought-reading, ventriloquism, conjuring, and " The Merry Little Japs."

Helmshore had one of Britain's first bus services. From November 1907 until July 1909, Haslingden Council ran an 18-seat Leyland bus to the village, but the service lost money and was withdrawn. The picture shows the bus outside the Commercial Hotel, which was the Haslingden terminus. The newspaper reports describe the arrival of the bus and its final departure.

EXIT THE MOTOR 'BUS.

The experiment made by Haslingden Town Council to give better communication than is afforded by the railway between Helmshore and Haslingden by establishing a motor 'bus service has been a frank failure, and in accordance with the resolution of the Town Council at the meeting of Thursday of last week the service was discontinued from Saturday night. It may have been imagination, but when the 'bus turned towards the tram depot on Saturday night after finishing its last trip it seemed wearied and worn. Only the strains of the "Dead March" were wanting to give it the finishing touch of decrepitude and decease. So ended an experiment that has cost much and brought little. Different experiments have been made with a view to increasing the receipts and reducing the working cost of the 'bus. Latterly the loss has been £4 10s. a week, the total cost being £13, and the receipts £8 10s. In addition to this loss, however, it is understood that the repairing of the 'bus has

been monopolising two-thirds of the time of Mr. Barnes Kay, the manager of the tramway department, and when the electricity distributing station at Prinny Hill gets to work, as it will do shortly, it will be impossible for him to spare this time. The damage done to Helmshore-road by the 'bus has not figured in estimates of the cost of the working of the 'bus, but it is a matter that should be taken into account, for the 'bus soon wracked up a road that had previously been the best in the borough. Some residents on Helmshore-road felt the 'bus to be a nuisance from its dust-rising smell-distributing, and in some cases house-shaking propensities, but these are not matters that may be transmuted into £ s. d., though to the people affected they could not fail to be things that count.

• • •   The truth seems to be that the motor 'bus has not yet been brought to such a stage of perfection as will enable the running of one to be a commercial success on a route such as that between Helmshore and Haslingden

"B2113."

HASLINGDEN AND HELMSHORE 'BUS.

THE TRIAL TRIP.

THE PRACTICAL JOKER AT WORK.

B2113 is the designation of the motor 'bus which is now plying between Haslingden and Helmshore, with a view to connecting the town with the village. One hopes the superstitious will not jump to the conclusion that there is something unlucky in the designation, but if they do they should be informed that the 'bus is behaving itself splendidly.

The 'bus was delivered in Haslingden on Monday morning, and on that day an official party made a trial trip on it from Haslingden to Southport and back. The 'bus is a single-decker.

On January 19th of the present year a deputation made a trial trip round Wilpshire and Whalley on a double-decker 'bus. That trip was full of "trials," and it was several times feared that it would include fatalities. A collision with Cock Bridge and breaking off one of the stone protecting pillars of that piece of county property was only one of the experiences, and as the trippers escaped from more alarming possibilities they congratulated themselves.

A memento of that trip of January awaited those who formed Monday's party as they arrived at the Municipal Offices, which was the starting point. In the grounds there was a large piece of stone, to which was affixed a card bearing this inscription:—

WARNING.

To motor parties, Town Councils, and other trippers. This stone is placed here as a memorial of the trial trip of the motor 'bus by the members of the Haslingden Corporation, 9th January, 1907.

To passers by, who wonder what I'm here for,
Don't laugh or jeer; just shed a silent tear, for
Know that once I stood at foot of Cock Bridge,
   Whalley,
Now here I lie, a Monument of Folly.

How the inscribed stone came to be in the grounds of the Municipal Offices, no one will admit to knowing, and all that can be said of it is that it was dislodged from Cock Bridge on January 19th, and undoubtedly is the particular piece of stonework that was found in the grounds of the offices about nine o'clock on Monday morning. The joke was heartily appreciated. A member of the Council who did not accompany the former trip turned up with a good supply of sticking plaster. Some who went on the former trip appeared to have other business on Monday. They did not present themselves as candidates for the trip.

B3455.

HELMSHORE 'BUS ON ITS FIRST TRIP.

COMFORT AND SPEED.

(By "BRIAR.")

The motor 'bus (B3455), acquired by Haslingden Corporation for passenger service between Haslingden and Helmshore, commences to run to-day (Saturday), and therefrom will run each week day. A trial trip was run on Thursday afternoon, and was viewed with complete satisfaction. The 'bus is a 14-18 h.p. B.S.A. It will hold twelve passengers, provided a few of them are somewhat below medium girth. Passengers enter at the front, and pay as they enter, the driver taking the fares so as to save cost of a conductor.

On the trial trip there were eleven passengers and the driver. The passengers included the Mayor (Major Halstead), Aldermen Witham and Warburton, and Councillors Anderton and Pilling.

Of these Aldermen Witham and Warburton and Councillor Anderton were three "survivors" of the hair-raising trial trip made on a double-decker motor 'bus by Corporation members, officials, and friends in January, 1907, which trial trip was full of threatened tragedy and accomplished comedy, with the result that any idea of the purchase of a double-decker for the Helmshore route was definitely lost somewhere between Accrington and Blackburn via Whalley. Even by comparison with the 'bus the Corporation ran on the Helmshore route from November, 1907, to July, 1909—by which time it had lost £495—the new 'bus is somewhat of a whippet.

The 'bus is scheduled to do seventeen trips from the Commercial (Haslingden) in a day. Seven of the trips are direct to Helmshore Station and back (by Helmshore-road). Others are to Helmshore, via Grane-road and Holden Wood, and other trips again are to Helmshore Station, then back to Haslingden by Holden Wood and Grane-road.

In order to give the 'bus a thorough test on Thursday, it was run direct to Helmshore as far as the lowest point of Station-road; then turned round to mount the stiff bit of Station-road as far as the level crossing; then turned round again, and taken along Sunnybank-road, and into Holcombe-road, and so on to Holden Wood, and back to Haslingden up Grane-road.

With Mr. B. Kay, tramways manager, at the helm, driving, and the Mayor at the rear, inside, time-keeping, everything went smoothly and well from the Commercial back to the Commercial, though just before it had been got to the Commercial in the first instance it had to be towed back to the tramway depot base for tuning up,

Haslingden's second bus outside the Bridge End Hotel in 1919. From Briar's description in the *Haslingden Gazette* of October 25, it became known as the "Whippet". It was one of the earliest, if not the first, one-man operated buses in the country. It ran for only four months, during which time it lost £315 and broke down frequently.

which occupied a few minutes. The passengers were much more comfortable than they were in the former 'bus, and it was evident there will be less wear on the roads.

Six minutes may be allowed for the 'bus getting from the Commercial to Helmshore Station, stage stoppage included. The route from Holden Wood to the Commercial was done in seven minutes, and this included the heavy climb up Grane-road!

The 'bus excited a good deal of interest on the road, but this was much more pronounced at Helmshore than elsewhere. Several stoppages were made to give people a chance of examining the acquisition, and at Holden Wood the Mayor called a halt in order to take the little company through the cloth bleaching works there, with which he is connected, and the visit proved interesting.

The route taken on the trial run went over two short lengths of private road—Sunnybank-road and a bit of Holcombe-road (Helmshore) from this point. It is understood that Mr. Porritt has been good enough to say that he will be prepared to come to an arrangement by which this route can be used regularly. If this is accomplished there will be an avoidance of Bowl Alley Lane—between Station-road and Holcombe-road—with its awkward turn and jolty surface, and there will be a gain to residents on the Sunnybank side of Helmshore and to Corporation income.

The circumstance that the 'bus holds but twelve passengers will prompt a question as to how it is assumed that traffic can be dealt with at busy times. The answer to that question is that the time-table allows ample time for a double journey being worked where only one is scheduled. Arrangements are being made with shopkeepers on the route to receive parcels for delivery by the 'bus.

Rose Queen Festival at Helmshore.

A PRETTY SPECTACLE

Helmshore was on Saturday afternoon provided with a capital spectacular fete in the crowning of the Rose Queen, promoted by Musbury Church Sunday School, in aid of the alterations that are being carried out to the school premises at a cost of about £800. The event was not well favoured by the weather, but in all the circumstances it is matter for congratulation that the interference of the weather was limited to a delay in the starting of the procession by about half an hour, and to a less crowd of sightseers than would otherwise have been the case. About £50 was expected to be realised, but this amount would probably have been doubled with good weather.

The village was en fete. Streamers hung across the roads, and flags displayed from many buildings.

The procession started from the school shortly before three o'clock, and was led by the Haslingden Temperance Band. It went along Holcombe-road as far as the Conservative Club, then past the Station up to Flaxmoss. Reversing at Flaxmoss House, the route back was the same until the Station was passed, and then the processionists made their way to Woodbank, up to Weir Foot on to Holme Field, kindly lent for the occasion by Messrs. Whittaker Brothers, where the prizes were distributed. Some quaint and humorous characters were included among the processionists, and these caused much amusement for the spectators. Not the least amusing character among this section of the procession was Mother Shipton with her husband, the "lady" having a false face on of tremendous size, while the husband had on a monkey's false face. Another, labelled "fragile," was a broken-down cart, drawn by a decrepit-looking horse, with two dummies on the cart. A rather curious character was a lad walking inside a pillar post-box, a label being displayed on the box, "Collections daily." "The Village Wedding" (after Luke Fyldes' picture) was also represented, with the "old fiddler" playing an air in front; and, following these, a cyclist had the wares of a shop on the top of his machine—pans, brushes, toasting-forks, wash-basins, buckets, etc.

On July 2, 1910, Musbury Church staged an impressive Rose Queen Festival, photographs of which appear on this and the following two pages. Above: The Rose Queen (Miss Alice Moorhouse) and her attendants at the Conservative Club. Below: The "Village Wedding" party on the Holme Field.

"John Bull" (Mr. William McQuilton) and "Britannia" (Miss Ethel Bentley). Above right: The lorry judged to have been the best in the procession - "Make hay while the sun shines" entered by Porritt's Mill. Right: Haslingden Fire Brigade in Holcombe Road.

OUR FUTURE M.P.'S

Above: Patriotism to the fore. The lorry representing "Britannia" in Holcombe Road. Right: A lighthearted comment on the "Votes for women" campaign.

A lurry representing "Britannia" had in the centre a young lady dressed as "Britannia," while at her side was Mr. McWilton, of Helmshore, the evergreen "John Bull." A troupe of girl Morris dancers also danced en route. Another character was Lord Roberts, represented by Mr. Robert Taylor. A lurry, labelled "Babyland," was interesting to look upon; and cyclists, with decorated machines, followed. One of the outstanding features was a lady who had on a dress entirely covered with picture postcards, while at her side walked a second lady, with her dress covered with advertisements. Included in the procession were a number of girls dressed as suffragettes, displaying cards "Votes for women." In front was a youth carrying a card, "Our future M.P.'s." In the procession also were the Haslingden Fire Brigade, with steam manual and fire escape, under Superintendent Harris; Boys' Brigade, Boy Scouts, a section of Ambulance men, cowboys, sailor boys, gipsies, haymakers, "Happy Japan," "Royal Maid," "Muldoon's picnic," "Garden party," "Old woman in a shoe," "Maypole," etc.

Bringing up the rear was the Rose Queen, Miss Alice Moorhouse, daughter of Mr. J. T. Moorhouse, of Flaxmoss, and she presented a charming appearance as she sat on the beautifully decorated lurry, dressed in a white silk dress, with a long dark velvet train, trimmed with ermine, and attended by page boys. On a lurry preceding her were her maids of honour, all of whom wore beautiful dresses. Mr. Arthur Moorhouse, the Queen's brother, rode postillion.

The crowning ceremony was prettily carried out. The Rose Queen (Miss Alice Moorhouse) was crowned by the Mayoress of Haslingden (Mrs. H. Worsley), who afterwards presented the Queen with a handsome Prayer Book. As representatives of different nationalities afterwards marched up to the Queen the band played appropriate airs. Afterwards "The Village Wedding" group gave a country dance.

The Queen had eight maids of honour, four page boys, four girl attendants, two train bearers, and crown bearer. The plaiting of the Maypole and the coronation were in charge of Miss Brandwood

and Miss L. Moorhouse, who had had the training of the children.

The prizes were awarded as follows:—Neatest gentleman cyclist, Mr. Fred Brandwood (Prince Charming); neatest lady cyclist, Miss A. A. Haslam (Summer). Most comical character on foot, lady, Mrs. R. Whittaker (postcards); gentleman, Mr. Ribchester, Edenfield; neatest gentleman on foot, Mr. Joseph Arthur Ashworth; neatest lady, Miss Addie Wilson (Flower Girl); special prize, Miss Emmie Barker (Flower Girl); most comical cycle, Mr. Kilsby (Edenfield); best lurry, the Haymakers (Messrs. Porritt's lurry); "Babyland" (Mr. John Downham's lurry); horse and lurry, "Happy Japan" (Messrs. Porritt's lurry).

The committee who organised the affair were Misses Brandwood, S. A. Cooper, Taylor, Downham, Woodhall, Leach, L. S. Whittaker, and Mrs. Oldroyd, Messrs. J. H. Brandwood, A. Whittaker, Fred Barker, Alec Pye, and Rd. Entwistle, with Mr. Edwin Hargreaves as secretary, and Miss L. Moorhouse as treasurer.

Church pageant 1911.

Pageant at Helmshore.

A PRETTY SPECTACLE

IN AID OF THE CHURCH BAZAAR.

A pageant in aid of Musbury Church bazaar was held at Helmshore on Saturday afternoon, and it attracted a large number of people and provided a pretty spectacle.

A procession in which about 300 persons took part was formed near the school, in Hollinbank, at half past one. In it were persons in character on foot, on cycles, and other vehicles; tableaux on lurries; and tradesmen's turnouts. Some of the features of the procession were particularly good.

Twenty-four young ladies, on foot, were dressed as Lancers. They carried lances and several of their number carried side drums. Miss Maud Taylor and Lieutenant A. S. Watson were responsible for this feature. There were morris dancers, girls and boys, who had been prepared by Mr. John Bradley. Joseph A. Ashworth typified Dick Turpin, and Jack Witham Robin Hood. Kathleen and Reginald Witham, dressed as Irish colleen and boy, rode in a donkey cart and represented Biddy and Patrick going to market. Other characters were taken from history and mythology. The Lancside Royal Standbacks were among those who supplied the humorous element.

Among the tableaux were "Summer," got up by the Misses Whittaker; "Autumn," got up by the Misses Woodhall; "Winter," got up by Miss

Cooper and Mrs. Ramsbottom; "A garden party," of little girls, in which the Misses Constantine figured; "A youthful wedding party," got up by Messrs. Moorhouse; a Red Cross waggon, with nurses and two patients; and "Flower Girls," got up by Mr. B. Eastwood. "At it should be," was represented by two tableaux on one lurry. Ladies were shown as having afternoon tea and the husbands as rubbing and scrubbing. This had been got up by Mrs. J. R. Dearden and Mrs. Fred Pye.

French Fisher girls, got up by Miss E. Woodhall, collected on the route. Members of the Haslingden Ambulance Corps were on duty on the route.

The route of the procession, which was headed by Helmshore Prize Band, was from Hollinbank to the White Horse Hotel, then down Free Lane, turning up Wood Bank and along Hollinbank to Weir foot, then turning back and going over the railway level crossing at the station and to a field at Gregory fold, lent by Mr. Jeffery Willan.

On the field there were numerous competitions up to half past five. Tea was served on the lawn of Mr. J. A. Witham's residence, near the field. The morris dancers gave dances at intervals. A doll dressing competition for men caused much amusement, particularly when Mr. Sylvester Witham appeared to make a remarkably good job of the doll he was dressing, and then put one of the articles of dress on the wrong way. A guide's race to the top of the Tor and back was done by the winner in 17 minutes 10 seconds, although the scratch man, Jack Berry, took only 14 minutes.

George V Coronation 1911.

HELMSHORE'S CORONATION BEAKERS.

On the occasion of the Coronation festivities at Helmshore, Mr. O. W. Porritt, J.P., generously offered to present each person who took part in the citizens' procession from start to finish with a Coronation beaker. It was liberally estimated that 1,200 of the beakers would be required, but so large was the procession—practically every resident of Helmshore was in it—that there was a shortage of 750 to 800, and these were distributed at the National School on Wednesday and Thursday evenings of this week.

HELMSHORE CELEBRATIONS.
THE WHOLE VILLAGE IN A PROCESSION

Helmshore, though a part of Haslingden borough, held festivities of its own. At six in the morning a Royal salute was fired. At nine there was a procession of the residents of Helmshore, Musbury, and Irwell Vale, who walked as one body without any distinction or separation. All taking part in the procession from start to finish received free tickets for coffee and buns and for tea in the afternoon, served in the schools, admission to the gala field in the afternoon, and a Coronation beaker (the gift of Mr. O. W. Porritt, J.P.). So enthusiastically did the village folk enter into the celebrations that there were about 1,800 people in the procession, and this left less than fifty spectators in the entire village. The shops and houses were well decorated.

The procession assembled at Hollinbank, and was headed by Helmshore Prize Band, followed by Ministers and Sunday school superintendents, the Mayor of Haslingden (Alderman Worsley), Alderman Witham, Councillors Shaw, Warburton, and Wilson. Then came girls, boys, ladies, and gentlemen. The processionists walked four abreast. Mr. James Walmsley was marshal. Hymns were sung under the conductorship of Mr. W. Moorhouse. The procession went through the village to the different Sunday schools, halting to sing at Tanpits, Piccadilly, and Wood Bank.

At Wood Bank Mr. Abram Constantine took the chair, and expressed pleasure at the entire unity and concord with which the celebrations had been arranged. The Mayor, in an address, said he was proud of the way in which both Haslingden and Helmshore were celebrating the day, and added that he was glad that whatever difficulties there had been at Haslingden had been amicably settled. The Vicar (Rev. J. H. Oldroyd, B.Sc.) spoke from the words, "Lest we forget," suggested by one of the hymns, and the Rev. J. Phillipson also spoke.

At noon coffee and buns were served in the Sunday schools. At half past one an adjournment was made to the Holme, kindly lent by Messrs. Whittaker Brothers. Tableaux, drills, dances, action songs, and the plaiting of the Maypole were given by children trained by Miss Brandwood.

Sports for children and adults followed. The prize winners were:—50 yards flat race for boys under eight: 1, E. Whittam, 2, Fred Mitchell. 50 yards flat race for girls under 8: 1, S. Tattersall. 100 yards flat race for boys from eight to 14: 1, S. Collins; 2, F. Haworth. 100 yards skipping race for girls under 15: 1, C. Tattersall; 2, Gladys Webster. 50 yards wheelbarrow race for boys under 15: 1, J. T. Kay and Jordan Entwistle; 2, Ernest Haworth and Rowland Honey. 60 yards three-legged race for boys under 15: 1, S. Collins and B. Malpass; 2, J. Kay and J. Hanson. 100 yards flat race for adults: 1, S. Collins; 2, T. Deakin. Ladies' 220 yards walking race: 1, A. Haworth; 2, E. Downham. 100 yards skipping race for ladies: 1, M. Tattersall; 2, E. Rostron. 60 yards egg and spoon race for ladies: 1, E. Downham; 2, A. Berry. Guides' race from the Holme to the Top of the Tor and back: 1, F. Mort; 2, H. Rostron. The prizes were distributed by the Mayor.

At nine o'clock there was a display of fireworks, and at ten there was a torchlight procession. The prize-winners in the torchlight procession were Mr. Fred. Hodgson (Arab), and Miss Schofield (gipsy).

During the afternoon the combined choirs of the village, conducted by Mr. W. Moorhouse, gave selections. Solos were given by Mr. H. Simms, Master J. Waite, Miss B. Leach, Mr. H. Cunliffe, and Miss D. Barker; Misses Stavely and Honey gave a duet, and Misses Hallam and Leach and Messrs. H. Simms and W. Crankshaw a quartette. Mr. Brooks Pilling was the accompanist.

The Coronation beakers presented by Mr. O. W. Porritt were insufficient by about 700, but those who did not receive them on Thursday will receive them later.

Villagers went to great lengths to make the once-frequent processions memorable events. This horse-drawn lorry was transformed into H.M.S. Victory for the peace celebrations of 1919. It is seen at the Conservative Club, members of which are wearing appropriate dress.

Page One-hundred-and-fourteen

TANK ADVENTURES.

Haslingden has notoriously ill-luck in regard to the weather on days set aside for outdoor functions. But we do not recall an occasion until Wednesday on which an outdoor ceremony was carried out to the accompaniment of a snowstorm, and a wind that seemed equal to cutting its way through anything. That was the kind of weather in which the Tank presented to Haslingden was formally received on Wednesday, in the Victoria Park. Quite a lot of things seem to have happened to the Tank apart from what happened to it when in France. It was a week overdue when it reached Helmshore station last Friday, and it had spent the week idling its time at Crewe whilst the Haslingden officials who wanted to give it a royal welcome were wondering where it had got to. What happened was that the Tank was addressed to "Harlingden" instead of to Haslingden, and then pushed North on the railway. When it reached Crewe the railway officials there, naturally, did not know any "Harlingden." It was just a coincidence that near Crewe is the village of Haslington, where many letters intended for Haslingden get, because they are wrongly addressed, only to be sent on to the place for which they were intended when the Haslington postal officials have hunted through their district, though often enough the Manchester officials spot an error in advance and sort the letter into the Haslingden bag. In the case of the Tank the Crewe officials knew the Tank could not belong to Haslington, though where it did belong to they had no idea. So they decided to hold it until it was claimed—just like a bit of lost luggage. During last week-end the Tank, then reposing inside the gates of the Haslingden Park, attracted many sightseers, particularly among children, and it soon became a thing of renown if not of beauty. When on Wednesday the trophy was formally handed over no military officer was present to carry out the duty. One had had to leave the town, and another deputed to take his place had either been unable to find or to reach the town. But Mr. F. Wilkinson, Major Halstead, and the Mayor (Councillor Anderton) among them carried through a ceremony befitting the occasion, and Mrs. Halstead christened the Tank "Hazeldene," using a bottle of lemonade for the purpose. And the Tank now belongs to the citizens of Haslingden, who earned it by their loyalty throughout the war in ever so many directions, though it is specifically presented to them in recognition of their help in financing the war.

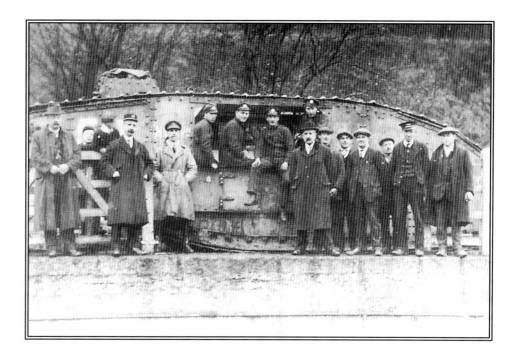

Helmshore escaped serious damage in both world wars, though loss of life among Servicemen during the first was very high. On the night of September 25/26, 1916, a Zeppelin passed over the village dropping a bomb on the golf course near the track from Greens Lane to Cockham. The bomb did not go off. Four incendiary bombs fell on the village during the Second World War, but only two went off - one in a field alongside Gregory Fold Lane, the other close to the steps in Bowl Alley. Two fell on Wavell Works (Middle Mill, now Airtours), but did not explode. The only damage was to an ARP warden's coat, used to extinguish the Bowl Alley bomb.

In November 1919, Haslingden received a tank in recognition of its contribution to the war effort. It arrived at Helmshore station (above) after being lost. It was taken to Victoria Park, where it remained for several years. The lower picture is of Helmshore members of the Local Defence Volunteers at the outbreak of World War II. They were photographed at Lockgate while marching to Rawtenstall for a parade.

The Silver Jubilee, May, 1935.

Mr. Ross Whittaker firing a 21-gun salute from the Tenterfield near his home at Top o' th' Brow. The first shot at 4.30 a.m. on May 6 woke people as far away as Ewood Bridge. The gun formerly belonged to William Turner, who ran Higher, Middle and Bridge End Mills, and it is believed to have been acquired by him after the attack on his power-looms in 1826.

The bonfire was lit on Musbury Tor by Alderman Jerry Lord, of Helmshore. It had been guarded by Boy Scouts from Sion Church.

"In Memoriam"

The
Stubbins — Accrington Line

Opened August 17, 1848. Closed December 3, 1966.

Old line farewell. Now useless you must lie
   In mute rebuke of those who let you die.
A hundred years ago we watched you come
   Arching the cliffs of Ravenshore and Lumb,
Slicing the hills and leaping every stream
   To lay the path of progress and of steam.
(How swift your triumph and how great the power
   Of trains that "flew" at 30 miles an hour).
Gone is that Age of Progress, gone the day
   When planners worked to make the railway pay.
Mocked and abused you were; but yet you showed
   One way to miss the chaos of the road.
The signal falls, the last train rounds the bend,
   The gates are closed, your life is at an end.

HELMSHORE LOCAL HISTORY SOCIETY

The closure of the Stubbins-Accrington line on December 3, 1966, was marked in proper fashion by the Helmshore Local History Society. Memorial cards with a verse and a picture of the Ravenshore viaduct from the *Illustrated London News* of September 30, 1848, sold rapidly to the passengers who boarded the last train for the journey to and from Bury. In the luggage compartment, Helmshore Prize Band played "The Excursion Train Gallop", which was composed in 1844 at the height of the Railway Mania. A large crowd gathered at the station to see the end of the railway service, the band playing "Auld Lang Syne" as the diesel train left for Accrington.

On the afternoon of December 3, a train hauled by two steam locomotives (above) passed through Helmshore carrying railway lovers on a special excursion. The trilby hat of one of the enthusiasts was blown off when he leaned from a carriage window.

FLOODS

The storm which struck Helmshore on the morning of July 18, 1964, turned daylight into darkness and was followed by floods which caused damage running into many thousands of pounds. More than three inches of rain fell in less than an hour. Huge hailstones smashed windows and blocked drains. Within minutes the streets were awash. Torrents swept down the steep hillsides causing the streams in the Musbury and Alden valleys to overflow their banks. The onrush of water in Musbury was said by those who saw it to have been a terrifying sight. Old weirs and much of the road between Carr Lane and Hare Clough were swept away. At the foot of the valley the flood caused immense damage at the mill of James Barlow and Sons which was built over the brook.

Flood water from the Alden Valley rushing by Woodbank Cottages. The photograph was taken by Mr. Tom Bottoms, who was living in the row at the time. The stream was at such great pressure that it forced up the thick concrete culvert in Sunnybank Mill yard. Higher up the valley the reservoir was filled with mud, which men using hoses took several days to remove.

Several passengers were rescued from a Haslingden Corporation bus which became stuck at Bridge End. The flood waters brought an eerie mist, which can be seen in the photograph of Bowl Alley. Hailstones float on the muddy waters and have turned roof tops white. The car in the above photograph was swept down from Tanpits and would doubtless have been carried much further but for the sewer pipes at Bridge End.

Mr. Fred Rumble was working at the works of TMM (Research), now Airtours, when the storm broke. He took the panoramic view on page 124 from an upstairs window of the building and from ground level recorded the scene looking towards Bowl Alley.

Above right is the flooded golf course at the end of East Street and right, Broadway at the junction of Lancaster Avenue and Brooklands Avenue.

The torrent that rushed down the Musbury Valley swept away the weir near Carr Lane, leaving behind the wooden axle of a water-wheel. The spokes had been cut off at the circumference, but the remaining pieces had come loose and were easily removed as the picture shows. The wood was charred, suggesting that it came from Hare Clough Mill, higher up the valley, and was used in building the weir. Hare Clough Mill was destroyed by fire in July 1873, when the owner, Mr. James Rothwell, was "devilling" through the night because of the good supply of water. The axle was rescued by the Helmshore Local History Society, three members of which are pictured. They are Mr. John Baron (left), Mr. Chris Aspin, secretary (standing) and the late Mr. Derek Pilkington, archivist.

The flood waters surge past Albert Mill.